HOW TO CATCH A SHARK

ANTHONY AMOS

with Contributing Author
KEVIN HARRINGTON

Published by Richter Publishing LLC – Tara Richter
www.RichterPublishing.com

Editor: Bonnie Young Crandall
Book Cover Design: Brian Taylor

Copyright © 2015 Anthony Amos

ISBN: 0615971199
ISBN-13: 978-0615971193

Disclaimer

HOW TO CATCH A

SHARK

TABLE OF CONTENTS

Testimonials vi

Dedication xiii

Foreword xiv

Acknowledgments xvii

Introduction 1

Chapter 1: The Making of a Shark Hunter 4

Chapter 2: Know Your Sharks 17

Chapter 3: Types of Shark Bait 33

Chapter 4: How to Catch a Shark 46

Chapter 5: Finding Your Congruent Shark 60

Chapter 6: Swimming in the Shark School 85

Chapter 7: Bringing Two Sharks Together 98

Chapter 8: Catching a Shark Without
an Introduction 103

Chapter 9: Catching the Wrong Shark 108

Chapter 10: The Bathe to Save Tour 114

About The Author 123

Contributing Author 126

Testimony 129

Special Thanks to Our Sponsors 131

TESTIMONIALS

Brian Ripka

Former President of Judith Ripka Creations, Founder and CEO, Ripped Fitness

Anthony Amos has become my business partner and great friend in record time. We are very much cut from the same cloth and get on extremely well.

We bounce around ideas about business and life with each other. This is not only effective, but extremely powerful.

I remember the first time I met Anthony when he was speaking at a KPI (Key Persons of Influence) event and thought, "Wow! This guy is either crazy or one of the most passionate guys I've ever met!"

Anthony is always upbeat. Every conversation is exciting. We have so many similarities in business and life, every time we talk is invigorating.

Anthony's the type of guy that when you need someone, he's there. He genuinely cares about people . . . that's why he has such a following and a great circle to play in.

As founder and leader in my own business, I am expected to pick up our employees when they're having a rough week. That's what leaders do. Anthony is the person who picks up the leaders, myself included!

Anthony loves life and the people in it. It's an honor to be his friend.

Roger Love
World-renowned Voice Coach to the Stars

No matter how successful you become in business, there are still some days when you need to hear a positive and energetic voice. When my tank is running a bit low, I call Anthony. His picture is in the dictionary of life next to the word "exuberant!" A little dose of Anthony goes a long way to recharge anyone's battery.

Anthony is very consistent and appreciates deep and meaningful conversations, the one's actually worth having. It's great to have a buddy like that.

I work with some of the most influential people in the world, and feel constantly inspired and blessed to teach and learn from these passionate and talented individuals. I enjoy creative people who live with intent and focus on what's possible. I always look forward to the next time Anthony and I can connect.

Brian Worley
Founder, Co-Owner and Creative Director of YourBASH!

I had the pleasure of meeting Anthony and his wife Rachel at the Knot Gala in NYC in 2013.

I was instantly struck by his confident, expressive personality and his ability to take his idea from conception to launch at the most prestigious wedding event in the U.S.

As the event coordinator for the Knot Gala, I worked with Anthony for a few months prior to establish a look and placement for his wedding bell concept. My communications with Anthony were always positive and inspiring and I could not wait to meet him in person at the Gala.

Since the gala we have joined forces with the "Bell" concept and I consider he and his family great friends! I know that whatever Anthony touches he puts his entire heart and soul into. He has a rare quality that inspired me to want to be a part of his venture.

Russ Whitney

Best Selling Author of Inner Voice: Unlock Your Purpose and Passion, Building Wealth, Millionaire Real Estate Mentor, *and* The Millionaire Real Estate Mindset.

I had the pleasure of meeting Anthony and his beautiful family at a Mastermind Group meeting, not long after they arrived on U.S. shores. I found Anthony to be very different compared to everyone else in the group . . . attracting my attention.

His personality is so much fun. He loves making sure everyone feels included in conversations. After spending any amount of time with Anthony, I find myself walking away feeling better and happier. His excitement for business and life are infectious.

Anthony has great business sense and an innate aptitude for connecting the right people together. He's become well connected very quickly in this country and it's admirable to see how his relationships and businesses have grown.

I am very close to Anthony and his family. We enjoy spending quality time together as it's always fun and a great laugh.

If you ever get the chance to spend time with this energetic Aussie, embrace it and listen to what he has to say. It's always insightful and meaningful.

Anthony is very true to himself and extremely authentic. I'm proud to call him my true friend.

Forbes Riley
Celebrity TV Host and Fitness Expert

Anthony Amos is one of those personalities that lights up a room and inspires everyone he comes into contact with. I first met Anthony not long after he brought the brand accelerator company, Key Person of Influence from the UK to America. Anthony was looking for some powerful speakers to help launch the brand in Tampa and having Kevin Harrington as one of his partners, Kevin and I have worked together in the infomercial and TV production business for years. He suggested me as the "female" voice of the USA brand, impressed by his passion and tenacity and was excited to be a part of this innovative speaking platform designed to foster emerging businesses and budding entrepreneurs.

Anthony and I have shared the stage a few times now and I must say it's never boring. This electric Aussie has got a monumental sense humor, is very down to earth and just adores his family - to me that's a beautiful, precious and priceless thing. I am particularly inspired by the personal approach Anthony takes to all he does and his ability to connect with a diverse range of personalities.

After meeting his well-spoken, well-mannered children and his beautiful, adoring wife, I became an even bigger fan, as it only further validated Anthony's true zest for life, happiness and family.

I've met many entrepreneurs and have personally done over $2 billion in sales on TV via home shopping and infomercials. I know character and personality types very well. With Anthony, it's so refreshing to see such a large personality with so much heart and integrity

For Anthony to be here in the U.S. for such a short period of time, he has accomplished things that others might take a lifetime to achieve.

He is an outstanding connector who brings the right people and Sharks together. Proud to be his friend and colleague. The world would be MUCH more fun with more Anthony's running around!

John Bartoletta

*Founder and Managing Member of UNATION, LLC,
UNATION Entertainment Group, LLC*

Anthony Amos and I met in 2013 when we were discussing a possible strategic joint venture with a company he brought into the U.S. From the start, I realized this was a man I needed to do business with, no matter what project was being evaluated.

Anthony exhibits qualities that have been left behind in today's business world. Integrity, empathy and his strategic networking ability are unmatched. This is a man that can talk to anyone and make them feel they are the most important person in the room because he believes in his heart that they are just that, important. He has an uncanny ability to put himself in their position understanding what their needs are. And because of that, he can connect them with the right people within his network who will engage and actually make a difference. Anthony's strategic networking skills are game changing.

Anthony's integrity is the foundation of his business and personal life. I believe his number one passion is people and the results in business and friendships happen in lightning speed like I've never seen before. This is a man that must be part of your life. I am honored to call him a business partner . . . but more importantly, I can call him my lifetime friend.

DEDICATION

———— ✦ ————

I want to thank and express my true gratitude to my beautiful wife Rachel and my three amazing kids Isabella, Austin and Aria for believing in me and sticking by my side through thick and thin. Without all of you, there would be very little motivation to have achieved the heights and success we have all created together. Your unconditional love and support has made me a better husband and father. I love you all to pieces.

—Anthony Amos

FOREWORD

by Kevin Harrington

———— ༄༅ ————

What makes Anthony different? He is real and open. With him what you see is what you get. As he says, he's always "ON FYRE." I like that. Anthony is always the cheerleader. It's a breath of fresh air because so many people wake up in a down mood. I've been around some of the greatest Sharks in the world—people worth hundreds of millions of dollars. Everyone knows who they are and aspire to be in business with them—but all some potential entrepreneurs can focus on is the negativity and the issues they're having with deals. Some people wake up with their glass half empty. Anthony's glass is always half full. I like partners with a positive attitude. I don't want someone negative always calling because something's wrong, like they're not feeling good or they slipped and fell. It's always some kind of bullshit with those people. These are the calls I stop taking.

If there's ever a situation where, as a Shark, I have limited time to do things and end up having to choose between a lunch with some ass that is going to complain the whole time or someone who's uplifting and excited about life, I'm going to go with the latter. In other words, if I can make four million dollars in four hours with a scumbag I don't like or somebody I like that's cool and fun, I'm going to take the fun route. Sharks look for positive things. They look for happiness. They look for a road to success that is easier.

Anthony knows where my sweet spots are; he knows my strengths and weaknesses. He knows when to involve me and when not to. He uses me as everyone should use a Shark—for my strengths. Other people use and abuse their Shark. In the long run, this will ruin the relationship.

If we're talking about a Donald Trump-type Shark, you have to understand how many hotels, how many deals, and how many things somebody like Trump is already involved in. If you come into a relationship with a Shark, don't try to command so much of his/her time. They're going to begin thinking, "This isn't working for me." It's important to make sure you know a good Shark has a lot of good deals and has a limited amount of time he/she can put toward any one deal. Utilize the Shark to the best of what they should be utilized for.

I had been in the franchising business for a long time when I met Anthony, so I knew to sell 200 franchises in a country the size of Australia was an amazing feat. I was super impressed with his track record and looked forward to meeting him. The first time we met was in New York. I had a line of autographs to sign and I saw Anthony, who was there to support our mutual friend who had told me all about him already, and suggested we go to dinner.

The fact that our mutual friend already told me about Anthony was helpful for him from the start. He wasn't one of those people waiting in line to snap a photo with me. I already respected him as a successful businessman, who knew what he was doing. When you get approached daily to do deals, you never know who could be coming in off the street. I begin to wonder . . . are they crazy? Have they run a business before? Do they know what's going on? I don't have time to waste with people who are not serious. I knew Anthony was serious to be able to grow a franchising system as large as he did in Australia.

ACKNOWLEDGMENTS

—————— ᘓᘔ ——————

I would like to express my gratitude to the special people who provided support, inspiration and valued feedback during the book creation process:

To my beautiful wife - Thank you for your love, support, honest feedback and encouragement! You are the one who allows me to be me and live my passion every day! I love you!

To Tara Richter of Richter Publishing and her amazing team with a special shout out to Casey Cavanagh. Thank you so much for your guidance and keeping me on track! Without you this book would still be in my head.

To Bonnie and Jay Crandall - This book would not be possible without your amazing editing and incredible input. You two are an amazing couple that we just adore to death. Thank you so much.

To Brian Taylor Graphic Design - Thank you for sharing your amazing talent! Every one of your cover designs was so amazing it was difficult to pick just one!

To Thom Sherk - Thank you for all your expertise in creating the "How To Catch A Shark" website and

SEO implementation, marrying all your creativity and contributions to the book.

To America - Thank you for embracing my family and me, and for making me a more complete and seasoned entrepreneur.

INTRODUCTION

T his book is a real life example of how you can catch a Shark in your industry, build businesses together and become great mates.

Coming from Australia to America was a culture shock for me, to say the least. For nine months I was an Aussie, still living in that culture. But the moment I made an adjustment to the American culture, my world opened up. What I share in this book are tools I have used to adapt to change and catch my Shark. My goal is to help you understand your unique value proposition, and create a change of mindset, which will result in knowing where to fish and how to catch your ultimate Shark.

I came to America not knowing anyone in the country. Within a year, I was doing business and hanging around some of the most influential business people in the U.S. To this day, it is still a mind-blowing achievement for me.

The moment an entrepreneur goes from "me" to "we" is when your Shark will appear. To catch a Shark is an experience fraught with danger, excitement and ultimately ultra-achievement.

To me, a Shark is the preeminent entrepreneur. They have valued relationships, are business savvy, and will add rocket fuel to your business.

A very close mate of mine shared his wisdom on being a translator, which reflects how I feel about what "mentors" do: translate and guide.

Catching a Shark is not the same thing as having a mentor. I find the word "mentor" a bit redundant for a couple of reasons. For example, when a student is mentored by an older person with "experience," the student brings enthusiasm and the mentor often lives vicariously through the student. So, it often becomes an even trade. Another reason I don't prefer the term is because as we grow up, we have many, many people that influence us in both positive and negative ways; anyone that shares knowledge and guides us is defined as a mentor. I prefer the words "guide" and "translator."

If this book was titled *How to Catch a Mentor,* I'm sure it wouldn't have the same effect. *How to Catch a Shark* is thrilling and exciting.

Before the recession there was what I like to call "free money." Everybody was an entrepreneur and the attitude was, "it's all about me." When the world hit tough economic times, the true entrepreneurs found a way to turn lemons into lemonade; the others went back and got a job. This is when the true entrepreneur adapted to the market and created a mindset of "we."

Teamwork and camaraderie wins the race. This doesn't mean you can, or should, be treated like a doormat; you must still have assertiveness when required.

Treating people with respect and being nice creates a wonderful and trusting environment. When you have the "we" attitude, you attract the most amazing and influential business partners and friendships you could only hope for. I teach my kids the philosophy: **it's nice to be important, but it's more important to be nice.**

How to Catch a Shark is a real life story that anybody can replicate. I'm telling you, if I can do it, anyone can. It has changed my life and my family's life forever in the most exciting and positive ways possible.

Being in several businesses with Kevin Harrington, my Shark, really isn't the highlight; becoming great mates is. We talk, text, email, and have lunches and meetings almost every day. How does that happen? I have known Kevin now for only three and a half years. And, let me tell you, what we have achieved in that time is nothing short of mind-blowing. The trust and mateship that has evolved is inspirational. I'm living proof that anyone can catch their Shark and not let it eat you!

—Anthony Amos

CHAPTER 1

THE MAKING OF
A SHARK HUNTER

Making the choice to move from the Land Down Under to the Land of Opportunity wasn't just a big decision; it was a life changing one.

For some people, moving to a different state is a big deal. Imagine moving to a different continent 10,000 miles away with a beautiful wife, three amazing kids, with only hope and faith in your back pocket.

Being the entrepreneur that I am, often I don't know how, I just know why. I'm always looking at the bigger picture, even if it seems impossible at the time. For me, building relationships and partnerships is the real secret of being a successful entrepreneur.

I started my career straight from high school with a professional rugby contract where I learned discipline, and a very strong competitive edge. However, I struggled with being told what to do.

Since the age of 15, I was hungry to run my own business. I learned how to leverage and delegate very early on. Growing up, my dad had a guy come and clean the pool at our house once a week. One day I asked my dad if I could do it and get paid instead. He agreed and gave me a trial run. I went to school the next day and asked some mates of mine if anybody wanted to clean my pool and then have a swim and fun afterward. I offered to pay my friends and that turned the job into a huge bidding war. At the end of the day, the pool got cleaned, we had fun, and everybody got paid.

I believe you have to love what you do, be passionate about it, love who you're in business with, and operate from a place of adding as much value to as many people as you can. Only then will the magic and money appear. If you wake up thinking about what you do, spend the whole day thinking about it, go to bed thinking about it, and then dream about it, you know you're fulfilling your dreams and on the right path.

When I started Hydrodog, a mobile dog grooming business, I was in my element. I maintained my discipline, competitive edge, and was my own boss. For me, being my own boss meant freedom; I could make my own decisions, even if they were wrong. I have found that making mistakes is a part of growing and appreciating the wins.

I started at the age of 21. I didn't know the first thing about business or grooming dogs.

I bought a second hand Hydrobath *(A Hydrobath is a bath specifically designed to wash dogs)*, fixed it in the back of an old garden trailer in my backyard, rented a mobile phone, put an advertisement in the paper, and waited for the phone to ring.

I put the ad in the paper on a Friday, expecting to get calls on Saturday. We rented a new mobile phone (you remember those big brick-looking contraptions!) on the same Friday and rang everyone we knew because we were so excited to have a mobile phone. However, no one actually rang us so we didn't know what the ring tone sounded like.

Saturday morning came around and our phone rang very early. I was still asleep and thought the fire alarm was going off! Half asleep, I answered the phone "G'day, Hydrodog, cleanest dogs in town." An old lady asked, "How much will it cost to wash my dog?" I told her we had a special offer for only $10. (This was back in 1994, so prices were much cheaper then.) I was so excited, I called my brother and told him we had our first customer and to be ready in 40 minutes. By the time I got to my brother's house, we had another eight dogs booked.

Since it was our first day on the job, we basically made it up as we went along. We met with the customer, took their dog and put him in the tub. As I reached for the shampoo, I realized my brother had brought dishwashing liquid instead of actual shampoo. We washed our first nine dogs in dishwashing liquid! Hydrodog has washed millions of dogs since our first day, using professional dog grooming shampoo of course!

We took Hydrodog from one dog-grooming trailer to the largest franchise of its kind in the world, turning over $10 million per year. I was one of Australia's youngest millionaires by the age of 28, and was building a wonderful future.

When I was 34 we sold Hydrodog for a record price that still stands today. We then immersed ourselves into real estate, starting construction on a $100 million Ramada resort in North Queensland. Unfortunately, the FGC (Financial Global Crisis) hit, and we all know what happened to the property game after the crash.

That was a defining moment for me to power on and make some life changing decisions. Starting from scratch, my wife and I put together a business model to replicate Hydrodog in the USA, found some investors and moved to America to launch Hydrodog USA.

Moving to America

On New Year's Eve, one of our last nights before leaving for the Land of Opportunity, we were watching the fireworks explode off the Sydney Harbour Bridge on TV. In that moment a huge gust of wind came through the back screen door and hit my face. I looked over to my wife and three amazing kids sound asleep, a tear welled up in the corner of my eye. I told myself, "These four people believe in me so much they are willing to move from our homeland, 10,000 miles away to another continent, with only hope and faith in our back pocket. I don't know how I'm going to pull this off, but I know I have to. Failing is not an option."

Once we made it to America, the five of us lived out of a suitcase for seven months going between California and Florida. As a family, I felt it was important for us to experience as much of the U.S. as possible in order to determine where we wanted to live as we didn't know what town/city or even state we were going to establish Hydrodog in.

For me, the hardest part of making such a drastic decision to uproot my family was not having the kids' extended family close by to visit. What I have come to realize is this experience has actually created a bond between the children far stronger than anything that could have been created by being with extended family. When you are always together, handling situations (both good and bad) and figuring out solutions to problems together . . . the experience creates a different type of relationship that can't be taught or bought. This truly was a life- changing journey I am grateful we took together. Because of this the five of us are extremely close.

Sometimes, you really have to go through something painful and challenging for your true self to turn up, and when it does, you can either be very proud or extremely disappointed.

Through luck, fate, or chance, I met the person who would become my new business partner with Hydrodog. It took over nine months to put the deal together. It dragged out for so long because although I was physically living in America, I was still in my Australian culture mindset.

We grew up watching American TV shows, but I was very naive to think that Aussies and Americans were culturally the same. I had no idea how different the cultures actually were.

We all speak English, but our cultures are extremely different! For example, when you get pulled over by the police in Australia, you get out of your car, walk back to the police car, and chat with him/her about why you were pulled over. If you tried the same move here, you could be shot!

The first time I was pulled over in America, I had almost missed an exit, so I veered off across the five-lane highway to grab it. Unknowingly a police officer was behind me. He put his lights and sirens on and pulled me over. I drove into a CVS car park, and thinking it was safe, I opened my car door to approach the officer as is customary in Australia.

I was greeted with a loud megaphone screaming, "REMAIN IN YOUR VEHICLE!"

I thought someone was playing a prank on me, as I'd never heard this before. So I got out of my car and the loud speaker yells, "SIR, REMAIN IN YOUR VEHICLE!" I started looking around finally realizing it was coming from the police car. I took one more step and the policeman busted his door open with his hand on his gun ready to point it at me, and he yelled, "GET BACK IN YOUR CAR WITH YOUR HANDS ON THE WHEEL!"

He was very serious as he approached my car. He asked me if I knew why I was pulled over.

I said, "Because I'm Australian?"

"NO," he said. "You veered across a five-lane highway to exit and I was right behind you."

Jokingly I said to him "I'm from the Bush! You know, the Outback in Oz and there's only one dirt road in and one dirt road out. This entire five-lane thing is very confusing for me."

"Driver's license and registration."

I told him my wallet was in my bag in the boot (trunk), so he let me out of the car to get it.

After he ran my license through his computer, he came back and said, "I'm letting you off with a warning today."

"Mate, that's great news," I said. "Can I take a photo of us together to show my mates back home?"

He told me not to push it!

The Cultures are Colliding!

What I do know about the American culture is they are very friendly to Aussies. Americans are like the Aussies' big brother. We know they are our number one allies, making sure Australia will always be safe. So we tend to play around with the Americans and can get away with a lot more than the natives.

I went to my first ice hockey game in Chicago to watch the Blackhawks play, and, *wow*, what a game! The whole experience was so exciting; I was "ON FYRE" the whole time! After the game, we were walking out of the stadium, and I saw the huge Blackhawk's mascot. It was about ten feet tall with an eight-foot wingspan. I couldn't help myself, I ran and jumped on top of the mascot and wrestled him to the ground. My mate raced over, pulled me off the bird and said, "Run!" I kept asking him why, and he yelled, "Because you can't tackle mascots in America!" Just as those words came out of his mouth, we saw the two policemen waiting for me at the exit.

The cops grabbed me and put one handcuff on. But before they could do the other I said, "Wait, wait. I'm an Aussie! We're allowed to tackle mascots at home!"

The policemen took me to the car, and asked my mate if that was true. He told them it was. The bigger, meaner copper asked me why I tackled the mascot. I told him, "I didn't see any signs that said 'Don't tackle the mascot.'" He told me it was just common knowledge, and I told him that where I come from, you're allowed to jump the fence at rugby games and tackle the mascot as long as it's in a fun way and not to be violent. I assured him I wasn't violent to the bird.

"Did you know it's a five thousand dollar fine, a life ban and two nights in jail here?" The other policeman asked me.

"Officer," I said. "If I knew that, do you really think I would have tackled such a prize bird?"

The bigger, meaner policeman said, "If we let you off tonight, will you guarantee us that you will not tackle the mascot again?"

"Just the bird?" I asked.

"NO! Any bird—I mean, any mascot in the country!"

"Okay," I said. "No more tackling mascots."

Just as I finished the sentence, the other policeman asked, "Is it true that kangaroos really run around front yards in Australia?" As I was confirming the truth in this, I knew I was off the hook.

After we shook hands, I gave them a couple of Aussie slang words to take home to their families. When we got back to the car, my American friend sat in silence and continuously shook his head, telling me that he had no idea how I was not in jail.

These stories are only a couple of many. I have now learned how far I can push boundaries, and I love to say while bumping my fists together, "The cultures are colliding!" when I really get into it.

My Australian nature, combined with my personality, is to have fun and to be honest. I know here in America if you say what you mean and mean what you say it goes a long way—with friendships and with business.

Coming to a new country is challenging at best, so you need to develop relationships with the natives to understand how the laws of the land work.

My methodology is simple; however, I need to stress that you have to be extremely disciplined. To achieve what I have in three and a half years is mind-blowing, which gives this formula the stand-alone credibility.

Learning About Shark Tank

Up until 2009, the concept of a Shark in business was thought of differently. The primary reference point was the wildly successful book – *Swim with the Sharks* by Harvey Mackay. Many could say he was the original Shark in business because he explained how to think differently in business in order to succeed.

However in 2009, *Shark Tank*, the American reality television series that premiered on ABC, clearly re-defined what a Shark is. As most of you probably know, the show features business pitches from aspiring entrepreneurs to a panel of potential investors called Sharks.

If one of the five Sharks accept the deal pitched, the Shark will take equity and partner up with the entrepreneur to get the product to market or successfully increase the business and hopefully take it to the moon! As of 2012, the show was averaging seven million viewers an episode, and was the most watched program on Friday nights in the 18-49 year old demographic. Re-runs are now being aired around the world to millions.

Kevin Harrington was an original Shark on *Shark Tank* when it first aired. Based upon watching and studying each of the Sharks, their personalities, business style and type of person, I decided I wanted to have Kevin as my business partner. But for me it was extremely important to understand that I did not want to do what most of the people on the show were doing. I wanted to do the complete opposite and I wanted to pick my own Shark. I didn't want to stand in front of a group to "spray and pray." Rather, I wanted to be in control and determine the right Shark for me.

Ultimately, Kevin was the one I wanted to get into business with. As the celebrity entrepreneur, he could take my business to the next level. However, I wasn't going to be like those guys on TV diving into the tank just to get raped and pillaged by giving over all my equity in exchange for the Shark's money. All I wanted was the Shark to open up the doors for me and create new opportunities. That's why I say it's better to catch the Shark rather than being eaten by one, feeling like you have to allow him/her to take advantage of you.

Want to know how I caught the Shark? Keep reading and I'll reveal the full story of how it happened.

SHARK HUNTER TIDBITS

1. Always come from a place of adding value FIRST!

2. Have faith in your own decisions and be willing to be out of your comfort zone.

3. Don't let a negative occurrence dictate your future direction.

4. Understand and learn the language of your new environment.

5. Be prepared to adapt to change.

CH🦈PTER 2

KNOW YOUR SHARKS

What is a Shark?

Most of you have probably watched *Shark Tank* or read *Swim with the Sharks*. But what exactly is a Shark and how does it apply to your business?

A Shark is considered a top feeder in the business world. They are the ones who have made it. Sharks run multi-million or billion-dollar businesses. A Shark recognizes the endless opportunities at their feet (which a majority never see). I like to say it's because they have Shark Eyes. Every single encounter of every day is an opportunity. For Sharks it's not about finding opportunities. Rather, it's seeing opportunity where others don't. It's sand sifting through and determining which deals are worthy enough to focus on or put energy/effort toward. How do they do this? Typically, it's determined based on the ROI (Return On Investment) and scalability.

Remember, that investment is not always just about money . . . it can be the Shark's time, talent or team resources. A Shark must look at what the investment is, what the return will most likely be, and the amount of time it will take to generate the return.

Understand that deals are pitched to Sharks on a daily basis because everyone knows this person can add enormous value to their business. Sharks are well established in the community. Their names come up in conversations, they are not always well liked, but they are definitely respected. A Shark can pick and choose which business venture they want to participate in. Examples of Sharks in today's world are: Warren Buffet, Richard Branson, Oprah, and Ted Turner. Aligning yourself with a Shark will always bring a certain level of prestige to your company and brand.

Knowing what type of Shark you need in the short, middle, and long-term phase of your business is critical. If you go after the wrong one at the wrong time, it can be detrimental to your business . . . costing you too much equity or not giving you enough "fuel" to grow your business.

To catch your Shark you need to understand what type of Shark you require. Then, put yourself in the mindset of that Shark. You need to see it first. What is the end you have in mind? Who are the people you need to strategically have in your business? Do your research to find out who you need, even those you think are not within reach. They can be within reach if you are resourceful enough to go get them. Just consider the idea of Six Degrees of Separation. If you know someone, they are going to know someone, who may know someone that can put you in touch with the Shark you need.

Different Types of Sharks

If you're trying to catch a Shark, you need to know what you're looking for. Examples are as follows:

Great White Sharks: Ted Turner or Donald Trump

Nurse Sharks: Warren Buffet

Hammerhead Sharks: Kevin Harrington

Whale Sharks (more likely to be older and very experienced with life): Harvey Mackay

The Great White Shark

When trying to get funding for your business, you are dealing with a Great White Shark. The Great White Shark is someone who will come in and invest the money while taking equity, but doesn't want to do a lot of work. You have to be careful with Great White Sharks so they don't take too big of a bite of your company. Ask yourself, "On top of the money, what else do they bring to the table, what is their expertise? Where do they add value?" Money alone isn't enough to create a successful business model.

As Richard Branson says, "Investors need to bring more than just money." When looking at investors, Branson suggests looking at what the investor is going to bring to the table and what level of input into decision-making they will require. The last thing you want in your business is to have an investor with different or conflicting values than yours. You need someone who will give you the freedom to run your business without questioning your decisions. Branson suggests you ask yourself, "Will this person or group give us the space and time we need to build a great business?"

When you meet with a Great White Shark, you need to bring your "A" game. You need to be highly confident, agile, ready for anything, and extremely nimble. The Shark may put you on the spot in the most unusual way. Not because they can but because he wants to see how you react. Your reaction determines your overall style in business. If you are radical, panic or freeze, it shows how you will react under extreme pressure. Be yourself and be on your game. Confidence is the key with the Great White Shark as there often is no right or wrong answer, only your answer.

Nurse Shark

The Nurse Shark is nocturnal and likes to hang in groups. The Nurse Shark could be likened to the silent partner type. They may invest as a group and look for comfortable investments. For this Shark, the numbers will be extremely important. They are not likely to invest in high risk, low reward ventures. They typically look for lower risk and moderate return. They look at the deal vs. putting their passion into the project. This type of Shark is not necessarily going to be a cheerleader and shout your brand to the moon. However, they may be a solid funding source for your company. This is usually a Shark you go after once you have an initial foundation for your business and are seeking funding to grow to the next level. That way the Shark can see what your past track record has been and what type of returns are possible.

When meeting with a Nurse Shark, subdued confidence is required. You need to have all of your facts and figures in order. Know your numbers inside and out. Be calm, cool, and confident. Have your presentation buttoned up. Bring supporting documents to show you are prepared to handle any question and provide an answer based on fact, not feeling.

Hammerhead Shark

The Hammerhead Shark is the most social of Sharks. They like to swim in large schools and have no natural enemies. This type of Shark will be beneficial to your business and brand as they have a strong social and/ or celebrity presence. Their name alone in association with your company and brand can attract other Sharks to want to invest or join the 'fun' in some way.

This type of Shark will want to buy into the potential of where the business can go, what's possible and how they can make a few introductions to their group of influencers to dramatically impact the business. When meeting with a Hammerhead Shark, it's about painting the picture of all the possibilities. Bring your gregarious social skills and be prepared. Know the types of circles the Shark runs in and be able to easily incorporate some examples of people into the painting of your picture of possibilities. This will open up the Shark's mind and creativity. The more potential the Shark can see, the more likely he will be on board with you.

Only approach this type of Shark when you are established and ready to exponentially grow. The right Shark can almost instantly catapult your business to new heights. They can create a brand, buzz and potentially generate sales almost overnight. I have seen companies that have literally gone from launch to multi-million dollar sales in less than a month with the right Hammerhead Shark on board.

The Whale Shark

The Whale Shark is the largest of Sharks! They are slow and methodical, do not use their teeth to eat and are not a threat to humans. They are graceful, confident and well respected. This type of Shark is very beneficial in your business as they bring with them a wealth of knowledge and expertise. This is the type of Shark that can influence your strategic plan and help take your business to the next level. They will bring in experience, great contacts and ensure you obtain all elements of the business model you will need.

When you meet with this type of Shark, be calm and collected. Show the path you have been on with your business and when you present the strategy for where you want to take the business, do so while seeking their advice. This Shark is a tremendous strategic ally to you and can help guide you through both calm and rough waters. Think of the Whale Shark as your guiding star. They are able to provide you with unwavering guidance and wisdom all based upon their vast amount of experience in business. This type of Shark is the one you want in your corner that can provide reassurance you are on the right path for greatness with your business.

Measuring Your Shark

We often hear of a Shark taking advantage of small fish and end up biting off more than their fair share. Many people assume that I would have needed to have 'given away the farm' in order to have Kevin Harrington be a part of my businesses. However, this is definitely not the case.

So, how do you identify and *catch* the Shark, rather than being caught by one?

My Shark, Kevin Harrington, was initially an introduction that added value for both of us. We've since grown into very close friends. That can only happen when someone is full of integrity, completely honest, and transparent. I have not met anyone who doesn't like Kevin. He is the "Prince of Business." He is the guy who gets it done, and is a man of honor. This was one of the most appealing things about Kevin to me. Having people like him in your life provides a measuring stick. I believe we are a direct reflection of those we spend the most time with. So aligning myself with such a person of integrity was extremely important. He's a very influential business patriarch in this country, and just happens to be a celebrity entrepreneur on top of it! I believe that sort of level in anyone's business can take them to the moon. Now, that doesn't mean everybody has to have a Kevin Harrington. It just means that you've got to find the right Shark in your business that can get you to the next level. It's about finding someone you are congruent with, can ultimately become friends with, and in turn, very strong advocates for each other—not just in business, but also in friendship as you move forward.

Before you set out to catch your Shark, you need to have a very clear understanding of the Shark you are looking for. When I was searching for my Shark, I considered the following aspects:

Measure of Success

I needed a Shark with a similar attitude toward success. Success is a loving family and the ability to 'give back' in some way to the community. Success can be something as simple as kissing your wife before she wakes up and dropping your children off at school every day. Success is waving goodbye to your children, and then seeing your child waving back until you are out of sight! Now that's success to someone like me. It means I've done a great job so far with my family, and they respect me. There are a lot of kids that get dropped off at school and race into the building wanting to get out of the car as quickly as possible. I feel swamped with an abundance of love every morning with my family!

I understood from Kevin's various philanthropic activities and his strong connection to his family that we were on the same page and very congruent in this area. I was once in a partnership where our measure of success was entirely different and the relationship didn't work. We found ourselves continually butting heads over long-term directional issues in addition to day-to-day operations and how we managed our time.

I personally connect to Ben & Jerry's Ice Cream business partnership and direction.

Ben Cohen and Jerry Greenfield were childhood friends. Not only did they share a love of food and ice cream, they also shared a love of community! They look at a two-part bottom line: financial and community give back.

Their congruent value system has enabled them to achieve enormous success. The Ben and Jerry three-part value system that guides their decision-making with a mindset of fun and gratitude:

- Our Product Mission drives us to make fantastic ice cream – for its own sake.

- Our Economic Mission asks us to manage our Company for sustainable financial growth.

- Our Social Mission compels us to use our Company in innovative ways to make the world a better place.

Everyone who knows me understands I live in a place of gratitude daily and I'm also a little (okay, a lot!) crazy and fun! It's important for me to surround myself with like-minded people who can share the journey and ride the wave in a similar way. I will always be the partner delivering good news or perhaps challenging news with a solution. Kevin is very similar . . . he lives in a place of gratitude and has a hilarious sense of humor! We have found ourselves in the middle of serious business discussions giggling across the table like a couple of school kids!

Richard Branson is often asked what the secret to his success is, and his overwhelming response is "fun." As he says, "If it's not fun, stop doing it!"

Transparent and Open Communication

I teach my kids to mean what they say and say what they mean. Too many people don't say it as it is in fear of offending, yet will speak badly about the person or whine about the situation to whoever will listen.

One of my first business transactions in the U.S. opened my eyes to the cultural differences regarding saying it as it is. In Australia, our business meetings end in some form of 'hand-shake' agreement and then the legal documents to seal the deal reflect exactly what was agreed upon in the meeting! Simple, right? No, not so much here in the U.S.! I like to do business with people who can say it as it is and not hide behind their attorney! It really boils down to trust and transparency. People know when dealing with me what they see is what they get.

If you're in a position where people are investing or purchasing franchises in your company or they are somehow contributing money or time, it's important to be consistent by sending regular updates to keep them abreast of any new developments.

With some entrepreneurs, their head is down and their arse (ass) is up! They work really hard and think it's the most important contribution. However, the people who invest in a company need the little touches. They need to be loved; they need to be kept in the loop. It's that whole thing about people wanting to be a part of a bigger plan. It's your job as the leader of the company to insure everyone is regularly updated and feels part of the bigger picture.

Respect and Appreciation for Others

It isn't all about the money. From my perspective, I don't chase the money first. I know that if I do the right thing and work hard toward results, the money will come. It is important for everyone on the team to understand the "why" of the organization. Whether it's for a particular charity or simply the long-term goal of the business, everyone needs to be on the same page and feel a sense of personal fulfillment with the direction and purpose of the business.

I see this in two parts:

In Business

Don't ever promise you're going to do something that you're not planning to deliver. Get out there and do it. Do the work and make it effortless for everyone else.

Set a standard for your team. Show the team how to get results by example. And, work with each team member's strengths. Get the results happening and bring it all back in. It allows them to stay focused while they are learning the skills that you as their leader are looking to demonstrate. When they see the team working together through your leadership, they not only begin to respect you, they also begin to trust your abilities. Even though you may be the founder, the owner, or the person driving the business, it doesn't necessarily mean you are the leader of the company. The leader in a business only shows up through results. Once you bring in the results, your leadership will be evident.

I believe this is one of the most important attributes to share in a business partnership: many people make the mistake of trying to micro-manage every aspect of the business and not respect the skill sets and knowledge of others. I believe in letting go of ego and allowing everyone to shine.

I recently consulted with a franchise system experiencing some struggles with strategic direction. I observed a situation preventing them from moving forward . . . they hired external advisors to help them sort out various aspects of their business from administration to production. However, when the findings of each advisor came in, they questioned it. They ended up spending a lot of money on many advisors until they found the ones who agreed with what they were already doing!! That to me is beyond crazy! If you take on strategic partners or a Shark, you need to value their opinion and focus on your own strengths and contributions.

Amongst his other talents, Kevin Harrington is an amazing creative thinker and very quick on his feet. I'm a very proactive and relationship-driven person who is loud and proud and gets it done. Our strengths and abilities are an unspoken agreement in our relationship. We both highly respect what the other brings to the table. We make a great team and throughout our various businesses, we continue to complement each other's strengths and limitations.

In Life

A true testament to a person's character is how they treat people. Whether it's the server at a restaurant, the gardener or the billionaire they are negotiating a deal with, each person should be treated with equal respect and kindness. Richard Branson, in his book *Screw It Let's Do It,* tells a great story of a cab ride he experienced in London. Richard was running extremely late and had not yet read the notes he needed for his meeting. The cab driver was extremely excited to have Mr. Branson in his cab and began to excessively chat with him. He asked if he would listen to his demo tape (a question that Richard gets asked every day). As much as Richard Branson wanted to say, "please be quiet and let me read my notes," he indulged the cab driver and kindly answered his questions. The cab driver then insisted Richard join him for a quick cup of tea at his mother's house which was on route to the meeting saying his mother was a big fan and would love to meet him. Not wanting to be rude, Richard agreed. Just as he was pulling into the driveway of the house, the cab driver played his demo tape. The words, *I can feel it, coming in the air tonight . . ."* blasted through the speaker. The cab driver then got out of the car and opened the door for Richard laughing hysterically! It was Phil Collins pretending to be the cab driver!

As Richard Branson says: "Respect is how you treat everyone, not only those you want to impress."

I once read a story about a man who didn't have a great start to his day. He burned his toast, spilled toothpaste on his shirt, stubbed his toe on the leg of the dining table, and then got a speeding ticket on his way to work. He was not in alignment with the universe on this particular day. He then went to a coffee shop to get his usual morning fix. When he walked in, someone handed him a pair of glasses to wear. As he looked through the glasses, he saw the life issues everyone around him was dealing with. Each person he looked at was experiencing something difficult . . . death, disease, job loss or heartbreak. He quickly realized his "bad" start to the day was really just that . . . a bad start. There was nothing that couldn't be turned around in a heartbeat. I love this story as a reminder to us all not to let the little things put us into a state of negative flow.

I like to think our temporary state of negativity is like taking the wrong off ramp on the highway. Our goal is to get back onto the highway as fast as possible to get us as quickly as possible to where we want to go.

SHARK HUNTER TIDBITS

1. Understand the type of Shark you need for your business, and pitch your deal accordingly.

2. Align yourself with a Shark congruent to you and who places a similar emphasis on success as you do. Success is more than money. Think about social conscience and family aspects.

3. Do what you say and say what you mean. Set the standard for the type of Shark you want to attract.

4. Don't bring anyone else into your negative state.

5. Recognize your negative emotional state as temporary, and quickly jump back onto the highway.

CHAPTER 3

TYPES OF SHARK BAIT

Having the Shark mindset means you are always thinking about the big picture. With every meeting and every deal, you're putting yourself into the shoes of the Shark. In order to find a Shark, you have to think like a Shark. You need to be swimming in the same tank and playing at their level.

When faced with the financial downfall due to the turn of the economy and loss of my property developments, the one thing I NEVER lost was my millionaire mindset ... even though my bank account didn't reflect the same! This may sound cliché but it truly was the one thing that differentiated me and kept me on the same playing field as those I wanted to attract into my business. I looked at my financial situation as a temporary state – just me giving an advance to the market for a short period of time! And I refused to let myself focus on what was. Rather, I spent my time focusing on gratitude and truly believing what I wanted was already in existence.

I needed strong influential business partners to help build the foundation required to position my business. Maintaining my millionaire mindset propelled me forward. I'm very good at living in the now . . . and that's why a positive mindset is so important. It gives you the ability to be consistently confident, "ON FYRE," and alive with enthusiasm.

Nice Guys are Shark Bait

Everyone knows the old saying, "nice guys finish last." I believe that saying is no longer accurate. It is gone. Today, the nice guy finishes first. Again, I love the statement, "It's nice to be important, but it's more important to be nice."

Before the economy crashed, financing was easier to attain and people could tap into it to venture out on their own. We were living in a society centered around "me," which meant people thought: "I can do whatever I need to do; I can employ whoever I need to employ; I don't really need to have strategic partners and give away equity, because I can afford to have who I choose to pay."

Then the economy turned upside-down. People had to change their approach to business. The true entrepreneurs floating to the top afterward had to think differently. They had to begin to think about collaborating with their suppliers, perhaps taking on financial strategic partners and teaming with other companies who shared demographics to more efficiently reach their market. The "wannabe" entrepreneurs got a job and went back to work while the true entrepreneurs readjusted their business models and stepped back in to the market. This new approach to business created a "WE" rather than "ME" mentality.

I believe the shift in the economy also humbled many people. The win-at-all-cost mentality changed to one of win-win.

The founder of Tires Plus, Tom Gegax, is a great example of a change in mentality that resulted in his life being completely transformed for the better. Tom's story:

> *"A number of years ago as the founder of Tires Plus he received what he terms a three ring wake up call. In the span of several months his 25-year marriage ended, he found a cancerous lump on his neck and his growing upscale tire store chain almost went bankrupt. He proceeded to get cancer treatment for his neck, therapy for his depression and took emergency steps to save his company from financial ruin. Several years later he was cancer free, his company was back on track and through intensive therapy he learned that he cared a lot more about recognition, money, success and winning the approval of others than really helping and caring about people. Tom realized he wasn't so nice. And so, Tom, who*

found his soul, became a different kind of person, a different kind of boss, a different kind of spouse. Years later this nice guy really did finish first, selling his company for a small fortune—sharing the revenue with lifelong employees and people who helped him get started decades before."

Businessman Barry Bergman, who has built two national multi-million dollar businesses and is the author of *Nice Guys Finish First*, credits his success to his nice guy attitude. "In all my business dealings, I've done my best to treat people the way I wanted to be treated in return. It's a very effective style, it made me a lot of money and I always felt good while I was doing it."

This is so simple and effective. It's probably a principle most of us grew up with, but so many lost on their way to achieving "success."

Cutting Your Losses - Nicely

At times you may have to consider cutting your losses. This is so important. It might be something that you decide to do because you start to understand you can't go much further; or maybe you've had a gut feeling; or somebody with more insight has explained to you that it's not going the right way. You have to be strong. You really have to let it go and jump on something else as quickly as possible.

Everyone's a leader until there's a difficult decision to be made. If I'm the owner and founder of a company, and although that's great in theory, unless I have to make those tough decisions during those tough times, I can't call myself a leader. It's going to happen. It's inevitable. Cutting losses is definitely more about getting personalities out of the way that shouldn't be there, removing people that somehow got involved earlier on, or slipped through the selection process.

It's better to make the difficult decisions, and to let certain things or people go so the company isn't brought down. I am such a firm believer in this, but I also believe these sort of conversations need to be handled with respect and kindness. There have been too many times that I've heard, "It's not personal, it's just business." I had a friend who was at a company for 10 years. For 10 years of her life, she was a single mum. She worked bloody hard for this company, and was really, really committed. She put the company first, even before her family. Many times, she didn't go to soccer games, or didn't go to school recitals due to her work commitments. So many times she put the business first.

The company was bought out, and a new CEO came in. After a month he brought everybody in and said, "We've had to make some cuts, and we are going to let some of you go." Later that day she was called into his office and he said, "I'm really sorry, you've been fantastic for the company and I really want you to know that we are going to give you a great reference, but we need to let you go. I don't want you to take this personally; this is just a business decision."

Now, think about that for a second. This was a decade of her life with her personal commitment to this company. How could it not be personal? So, I don't believe that people can say in one breath, "It's not personal, it's just business." The two are too intertwined. Business and personal is one thing to me.

Please understand . . . if you're going to go all out and get the best team for your company, you have to get personal with them. You have to go out and have dinner and understand their "why." It's about getting into the thick of it and getting to know each other personally. So when you're in the trenches, and you have a really tough day and you need to count on everyone, you know they are there for you. It has to be personal.

A Personal Story: Landing the Wrong Shark and Letting Him Loose

During my first two years in the U.S., I was able to land five very different Sharks. While Kevin Harrington is the only celebrity TV Shark, the others are definitely Sharks in either their industry or in the general business world.

The number one thing I want to stress here is that while we refer to *bait* and *capturing* a Shark, it's really all about providing the value necessary to attract the Shark you are fishing for. The predominant reason I have been able to attract and maintain relationships at this level is because I am always ME!! Authenticity and integrity are the ONLY way you will be able to live in these waters.

The very first Shark I met was my most challenging. Our value systems were not in alignment, but we both needed one another (for different reasons). I was able to add value to his business with a unique product that he wanted, and he was able to provide me with the infrastructure I needed coming into a new country.

The Problem

This Shark was looking to corporatize the business, not franchise it. I already knew what I was doing from my experience in Australia—I just needed the funding and infrastructure to get started. Unfortunately, he wanted to have a hand in the everyday operations, and it led to so much conflict I eventually sold my share of it to his company and left our partnership for good.

The worst part is I knew this was going to be a problem from the get-go, but I tried to ignore it. I thought maybe this Shark would bend a little bit and learn from me (Surprise #1: he didn't). And I hoped I'd be able to change myself to be more accommodating (Surprise #2: I couldn't). My gut told me from the beginning it wouldn't work, but I didn't listen. Oops.

What I Should Have Done Instead

I should have searched for a Shark that more closely matched my values, goals, and process. Most importantly, I needed a high-profile franchiser, not a hands-on investor. That's one of the reasons Kevin and I get along so well—he's a great franchiser, and he loves it when all the news I have for him is, "Hey, Kevin, things are still going great!"

Shark Sweet Spots

Yes, Sharks have sweet spots. You know, those little nuances that can be leveraged to garner even greater results. Get to know those sweet spots! Let me give you an example. On *Shark Tank*, one lady said she was gunning for Kevin because she had a kitchen product. She knew what Kevin's sweet spot was . . . and it was kitchen products. She was going to catch Kevin and Kevin actually wanted the deal.

Kevin O'Leary, also on *Shark Tank*, during this time was saying products aren't a business. He said he wasn't interested in products. If the same lady tried to get the deal with Kevin O'Leary, it wouldn't work since kitchen products aren't his sweet spot. This is the wrong way to approach that Shark.

Research the Shark that you're trying to catch, understanding those sweet spots. I have discovered Kevin has 10 or 12 sweet spots. Other Sharks may have only one. For example, some investors and/or Sharks don't do startups. They're too risky. They only invest where there are healthy profit margins. For others, a healthy profit margin means not enough money is being spent on advertising . . . advertising spending is kept low to make a big profit. Do you think Facebook started that way? No. Facebook doesn't care about the immediate profit. They're all about exponential growth of users.

Let's take a look at some of Kevin's sweet spots:

1. Healthy Profit Margins

2. Exponential Growth

3. Good Cash Flow

4. An Industry Ripe for Acquisition

Even if you have the greatest product, there are some Sharks that, unless you have a strong and experienced management team, aren't interested. If you give the best pitch in the world to Robert Herjavec, also on *Shark Tank*, he loves it. But if you don't have any experience or an experienced management team behind you, he's not going to invest in the deal. He'll question what's going to happen to the money if the management team isn't experienced.

Ask Yourself These Questions:

1. Do you have any of your own money (bootstrap capital) in it?

2. Is it a unique product or service?

3. Does it solve a problem?

4. Do you have a new distribution system?

5. Is there technology, IP or patents? (O'Leary is huge on patents.)

6. Does it fill a hole in the industry?

7. Does it have quick ROI (Return On Investment) and break even?

8. Does it have a proven test market?

9. Is it scalable?

The quick ROI is something nobody has offered on the *Shark Tank*. Here's how I see it going. "Hi Sharks, I want a hundred grand and this is what I'm willing to do for it. I'm willing to give a quick ROI such that 100% of the profits go back to you, the Shark, until you get all your money back, plus 20% return on your investment."

You're basically telling the Shark, with that pitch, is he/she gets an interest in your company for the rest of their life, a 20% ROI, and you're going to accelerate their financial payback. In six months they'll get all of their money back. There's virtually no risk. They get a quick ROI and then a carried interest for the rest of their life. Your main focus should be, "What's in it for the Shark?" Put yourself in the Shark's shoes. Why would they even listen to your pitch? Why should they give you the time of day? You better tell them what's in it for them.

One of the most important things is to understand is the person's strengths and weaknesses and abilities to contribute. I think I'm very sensitive to certain kinds of people that I do business with. I don't want to take too much of their time, or command too much.

Make sure you're not expecting too much from your Shark, or it's not going work.

For Mark Cubin, who's also on *Shark Tank*, his line is, "You're the expert. You go do it. Don't call me every day. Remember you're the CEO of the company. I invested in YOU."

You can't expect a Shark to be on-call all of the time. For example, Kevin Harrington invested a half million bucks into a lady's product on *Shark Tank*. She called Kevin on a Tuesday and said, "Hey, I've got an event this weekend and I'm expecting you to be there." She lives in San Francisco and Kevin lives in Florida. It was Tuesday and she wanted him there on Friday. This was the first he had heard about the event. She was expecting Kevin to spend three days in a booth at a trade show. "WOW" is what I said when I heard the story.

When I asked Kevin what her reply was when he questioned her last-minute move, he said the entrepreneur told him that it was a last minute thing, and she got a good deal on the booth, and she couldn't afford it until the Shark came in with the money. She went on to say that since she and Kevin were partners, he should be there. Needless to say, Kevin didn't attend and it wasn't long before he sold his shares in her company.

The person catching the Shark needs to realize that a Shark has many other things happening. You need to have an understanding of who's doing what and how it's all going down on a day-to-day, a week–to-week and a month-to-month basis. Come to an understanding of how often you should meet with your Shark. Is it going to be a couple times a week? Or, is it going to be three or four times a month or a year?

Each Shark is different depending on the level of involvement they are needed for. It's one thing to keep them in the loop on things, but don't bog them down to the point they don't want to be your Shark anymore because it's taking too much of their time. At the end of the day, the Sharks look at the businesses assessing how much time it will require and what his/her upside will be.

Your Shark might not be eager to spend three days at a trade show. He's counting on you to build the business. He's already made the investment. He already owns a piece of the company. If you had *The New York Times*, *The Wall Street Journal,* and *USA Today* along with the film crew of *The Tonight Show* wanting to interview your Shark at the trade show, that is a different story. Use the Shark's time appropriately.

SHARK HUNTER TIDBITS

1. The nice guy finishes FIRST! It's nice to be important, but it's more important to be nice.

2. Choose your Shark wisely. Make sure the relationship is congruent.

3. If things don't go as planned, never burn a bridge.

4. Make a list of what is important to you in a Shark and be clear on the non-negotiables.

5. Understand your Shark's sweet spots and target your pitch to add value first.

CHAPTER 4

HOW TO CATCH
A SHARK

❧❧

Establishing a brand in a new country is a difficult task regardless of whether it was well known or not in its home country. When I was in the process of putting together my team for my current franchise, I decided I needed a 'Hammerhead Shark' to promote my brand to the masses. I had already put together a great team of strategic partners, but the one thing missing was the person who that could get me in front of the movers and shakers of the industry.

A Personal Story: Where Do You Swim?

You never want to be the most intelligent or wealthiest person in the room! I think I really began to understand this concept and the importance of social circle at the age of 17.

I was raised in small country town in NSW, Australia

called Tamworth. I started playing rugby at the tender young age of five, and my biggest goal was to one day play professional football for Australia. During my early high-school years in Tamworth, I was recognized as a footballer with promise and made the local A-grade football team. I was in my element playing a game I loved, at an elite level for a 16-year old, in the town I was raised in, surrounded by my family and friends.

As great as this was, my burning desire at that age was to play for Australia. I knew that in order to do so I needed to surround myself with the cream of the crop in schoolboy rugby league players. I had heard about an elite rugby league, High School on the Gold Coast of Queensland, that were winning the schoolboy's national competition—the next level. I knew this was the school I needed to be in to take my game to the next level. Surrounding myself with high-caliber players would push me to improve. So, I transferred. And it worked. During the first year at the school, I made the Queensland side and shadowed for Australia! That year, it was the first and only time in history that a student had changed states and made the Queensland side! I experienced the benefits of jumping out of my comfort zone and surrounding myself with people who would challenge me.

As I look back, I recognize this was the year I also *caught my first Shark*! This Shark was presented in the form of a lovely 60 year old headmistress named Mrs. Ginenen. Although she looked sweet and harmless,

Mrs. Ginenen was a formidable taskmaster, renowned for her discipline and no bullshit approach. Nothing got past this woman!

While I was "ON FYRE" with football, there were certain teachers and subjects that could not hold my short attention span . . . and if I was going to continue to play, I also needed to keep my grades up. One particular teacher I was struggling with happened to be close friends with the headmistress, Mrs. Ginenen. My strategy was to appeal to Mrs. Ginenen to help me find the sweet spots and give me some guidance to be more in alignment with this difficult teacher. Little did I know that I was hitting Mrs. Ginenen's sweet spot. We struck up an amazing friendship in the process. Instead of sitting through a double period of a subject that I couldn't stand, I ended up sitting in Mrs. Ginenen's office, drinking tea and talking about life.

She is still very dear to me today and was there to welcome my wife and all three of my children into my life.

The lesson here is simple—if you're the smartest person in the room, you're in the wrong room!

Meeting Kevin Harrington

Meeting the right people is all about pursuing specific environments. You've got to get creative, especially if you're on a very tight budget or no budget at all. Make sure you're in a position of adding value . . . whether it's your personality, your contacts, or something unique that people want more of.

When I wanted to meet high-profile people, I knew being part of a prestigious mastermind group would place me in their environment. One particular group I wanted to join had an annual fee of $25,000. I wasn't in a position to pay out that amount of money, so I approached the guy organizing it and said, "If you give me the opportunity to become an annual member, I'll bring two paying customers to the table to become part of your mastermind group by being a raving fan." He agreed and that was the door opener for me. I had evened the playing field in order to meet the high-level business contacts I needed. It's all about finding the right situations to meet the right kind of people.

In this instance, the strategic partner was the guy who owned the mastermind group. He was doing something with a lot of other very successful and wealthy guys, and I wanted to be a part of it. I had to work with him rather than paying the money and creating a transaction. I was resourceful. I brought in two people as promised and created a high-level relationship and amazing friendship with the founder of the organization.

I was introduced to Kevin Harrington believe it or not, through this high-end mastermind group I creatively worked my way into. Through this group I met an amazing bloke who provided the most important thing I needed to have when catching a Shark like Kevin Harrington . . . a great introduction. Unbeknownst to me at the time, he happened to be a good friend and business partner of Kevin's and arranged an introduction. Before I even met Kevin, he painted me as this crazy Australian guy who was very successful, and had founded a franchise system that was just amazing. Because Kevin heard about me from a trusted source, he wanted to get to know my products and me. Now, at the time, I didn't know the connection my new friend had to Kevin. I authentically befriended this bloke as he was someone I felt instantly congruent with and has since become one of my greatest friends. He is someone who always provides great advice from spiritual to business for my family and me.

It's all about forming alliances and friendships, adding as much value as you can. Even the playing field so that when you get an introduction to your Shark, you are instantly differentiated from the hordes of people who pitch to him/her on a consistent basis. You come recommended.

I teach my kids all the time to never follow the crowd or they will always end up at the exit. You've got to do the opposite of what everyone else is doing. In every situation I always think, "What is everyone else doing and what is it that I can do differently to stand out?" That happens to me every day.

When you follow the crowd, you will achieve the same results as the crowd. Everyone doing the same things are getting the same results. Choose the path less traveled. At times it can be the more difficult choice, but most times it pays off. If it were easy, everybody would be doing it. Remember, you want to stand out, not blend in. Do the things other people aren't.

Live outside the box . . . don't just think outside the box. That's the key. When someone asks if my glass is half full or half empty, I want to know who's pouring the drink.

How to Stand Out from the Rest

Steve Jobs said, "every new business pitch should do three things: inform, educate and entertain." I would like to add another and that is to transform – to solve a problem.

I am a firm believer in the idea that people invest in people, not only products or services. I knew that for a 'Hammerhead' to be remotely interested in my business and me, I had to stand out from the rest. I had to have my pitch down pat and be able to reel it off at a moment's notice. Not only did I need to know my pitch, I needed to know it in a way that could be easily converted depending on the environment.

The way I would deliver my pitch to a group of business associates in a conference room is different than the way I would deliver it at the bar to a bunch of blokes. However, the message and enthusiasm are always the same . . . just the language of the story varies.

Your pitch should be a story you can easily tell. Just as you can easily talk about the great qualities of your spouse or children, your pitch should be just as organic and not sound manufactured.

A Personal Story: Know Your Pitch's Audience

In Australia, business lunches are accompanied with at least one or two cold beers—especially Friday late lunch. So when I offered to buy the first round of drinks in America, and came back with Patrón shots and beer chasers for the table, I expected a completely different response than the one I received! To make a long story short, I ended up taking all the shots myself and having quite an afternoon at the office!

The point of the story is: it's important to understand the personalities you are around and the driving forces of your audience in order to have a real impact (and protect your liver). As I've mentioned previously, be your authentic self. But, always be mindful of others. In the above example, I should have asked if everybody wanted a drink instead of assuming it. Again, it was a cultural thing, but I should have thought of them first.

Creating the Perfect Bait

In order to catch your Shark, start by creating the perfect bait. Last year there were approximately 50,000 entrepreneurs auditioning for *Shark Tank*. It is quite a process to whittle that number down to about 300 aspiring entrepreneurs actually chosen to appear on air, with an opportunity to pitch their product. The process is long and involves the following: a casting call, then submission of a more formal application (disclosed information), a video describing their business (marketing pieces, etc.), and finally, an even more in depth application providing the numbers for the business.

Of the 300 progressing to the live show, approximately 30 entrepreneurs got their Shark and landed a deal. How did the first batch of people get through? It all boiled down to one thing: creating the perfect bait. The following 10 steps are written by one of the original Sharks, so pay attention!

SHARK BITE

by Kevin Harington

10 Steps to Creating the Perfect Bait

1. Attention Getting Statement. Open with something dramatic to make sure they're listening.

2. Show how your business or product is a Mass Market Proposition. How scalable is the business?

3. Solve a Problem. How does your business provide solutions to customers? What are the benefits of your business or service?

4. Uniqueness. Show how and why you're different. Is there any intellectual property within your business?

5. Magical Transformation. How does your product or service do something magical? *The Biggest Loser* TV Show is a great example. Contestants can go from 400 pounds to 160 pounds.

6. Visual Demos. Can you show something demonstrable or multi-functional? Visuals can be very powerful.

7. Testimonials. Do you have powerful testimonials? There are four kinds:

   a. Consumer/User

   b. Professional - Such as doctors, lawyers

    c.   Editorial - Newspapers, TV News

    d.   Documentation - Clinical trials, testing

8.   Celebrity Endorsement. Can you tie in some kind of brand seal of approval? Or an action plan on how you are going to get "Google Famous?"

9.   Your Track Record. Your experience is key, but also the management team you've assembled. Do you have a powerful Board of Directors? Who's on your team?

10. Financial Projections. What's the capital needed? Competitive landscape, risk analysis and bottom line. Talk about how successful and how much money the business is going to make!

Practice, Practice, Practice!

Practice your bait and always be prepared. Know the outline of the bait just in case you get the chance to use it. You don't need to have it completely memorized, but you have to know the outline. Practice in front of a mirror. Practice in front of your spouse or whoever is willing to listen. Practice as if you were going on TV.

I use what is called the "memory pegs tree list" in order to remember things. This involves 20 specific items allowing me to word associate and remember any list, any characteristics/details about a person and always be prepared. If you want to learn more about this amazing technique, simply go to:

www.HowToCatchAShark.com

and I'll show you my Shark Hunter trick. It's really all about remembering facts important to the Shark.

Another brilliant Shark, Richard Branson, has these tips for a great pitch:

1. Avoid wishy-washy language like "we hope that . . ." or, "with some luck we will . . ."

2. Your pitch needs to be clear, concise and something that investors can easily understand and repeat.

3. Give a clear explanation of why your business model will be sustainable and be

able to pull through technological changes and markets shifts.

Tailor Your Bait to the Type of Shark You are Seeking

Start by doing your research. Discover the hot buttons of your particular Shark. What are their sweet spots? What are the interests of the Shark you want to catch? The "I'm going to donate the money to charity" pitch doesn't always work. Some people assume the Shark will donate the money to charity. No. They have enough charities in many cases. That might work for people, but Sharks like Donald Trump are about making money. The bottom line is . . . he wants the money in his pocket.

People come to Kevin Harrington all the time requesting little favors. One example is Bill. He met Kevin's wife and over dinner, she mentioned how much she loves the Bahamas and the Atlantis hotel. Bill wanted Kevin to be a speaker for him, but didn't ask him directly to speak. Instead, he bought Kevin and his wife an all-expense paid, round-trip vacation to Atlantis for three days and three nights. It included everything: the hotel, food, hotel transfers, limos and airfare. All he wanted from Kevin was 30 minutes of his time to speak in front of a crowd. And if Kevin sold anything, he got 50% of the profit. Bill knew one of Kevin's sweet spots was his wife. He used this knowledge he gained from Kevin's wife to seal the deal. Bill sent an email to Kevin, and of course Kevin forwarded it to his wife. Her response? "Oh my God. You're going to do it . . . I hope!"

How did he get the Shark? He appealed to what Kevin loves . . . his wife. The point is to know what the Shark wants/likes. As I said earlier, do the research. Find out what they do in their spare time. I mentioned Donald Trump builds golf courses all over the world. If you've got a golf angle, you've just tapped into his sweet spot and hot buttons. You should know what floats their boat. What gets them excited? What motivates them? It's not always just about the money.

SHARK HUNTER TIDBITS

1. Put yourself in the right environment to meet the Shark you need. Be creative to get your foot in the door of high-end exclusive places and maintain a mindset consistent with the Shark you want to attract.

2. Be considerate of your Shark's time. It's extremely valuable.

3. Understand the type of Shark you need in your business by assessing your current team and determining one Shark type that could benefit your business and growth strategy.

4. Know your pitch and be able to adapt it to your audience – always deliver with passion and enthusiasm remembering people invest in people.

5. Do everything possible to stand out from the rest – be the person that people want to be around and invest in.

CHAPTER 5

FINDING YOUR CONGRUENT SHARK

❧❧

When I first moved to America I attended some business seminars and networking events with so-called 'gurus' of different industries. The one thing that really stood out for me and was consistent throughout all the events was the amount of people in the room who immediately placed a lower value on themselves than that of the people on stage. These are the people who line up to take a photo with the speaker or get an autograph of someone they aspire to be like. Rather than using the 1-minute or so they may have with that person to make an impression, they choose to follow the crowd and just get the photo!

Avoid Common Mistakes:

Congruence

Sharks can only help if they are congruent with you. Otherwise, you're not going to be able to get the value, or the direction you're after. What exactly does this mean? For 20 years I've been working really hard to discover what congruence looks like for me. I've embarrassed myself. I've put myself in situations I knew very few people would. I quickly knew I had to go to those extremes to understand different personalities, and often, when you find a person whose "values" align with yours, you've found someone you are congruent with.

Often I hear people say certain relationships just "fell out" or "didn't work out." What this really means is they were not congruent in the first place. I think women have the instinct of knowing whether or not they are congruent with someone naturally. Guys have to work a lot harder.

Congruence is not necessarily about having similar interests and recreational things in common. It's their core value system that is important . . . to make sure it is a reflection of your own. Our core value clarifies who we are, what we stand for, and why we live and do business the way we do. The one thing that solidifies our core values is the consistency in which we act on them. The important concept is, once you realize your congruency is really strong, you're off to a good start. I can honestly say when I walk into a room I can feel who I am congruent with as the conversations start. Once I realize this, I will add as much value as I can. They might not even be the strategic partners I need. Simply, they may be able to steer me in the right direction, acting as a conduit for a future strategic partner. A great example of this person to me is the guy who introduced me to Kevin.

Mindset

It always comes back to mindset. Set yourself apart from the crowd and at the level of your desired Shark to communicate what speaks to them, giving you a greater chance of being heard.

Too many people follow the crowd. I always do the complete opposite of what everyone else is doing and consistently think about how I can be different in every environment I am in. People often ask me how I maintain a positive mindset all the time. It's discipline. I make a conscious choice every day when I get out of bed. You have a choice as well. You can choose to make every day the greatest day in the world. Or you can choose to make it the worst day, or something in between. Bottom line, it's your choice. A positive attitude and an attitude of gratitude is what becomes truly contagious. Your positivity becomes infectious and people will want to be around you more often. I have people who just want to hang out because of my positive energy. The kids have other children always asking if I'm going to be at the next field trip . . . because I'm not like all the others. I'm positive every day, by choice.

In business and especially when trying to catch a Shark, it is so important to be positive. Even when life seems to be at its worst, remember there are people suffering from hunger, lack of water and/or shelter somewhere on this planet. Every one of us is extremely fortunate and blessed. Choose an attitude of gratitude every day and know that whatever is happening in your life at a particular moment is meant to be and will take you on a new journey or path that will usually generate something greater than what you even thought possible. That's been my experience in life and is also the experience of every one of my friends. Yes, every one of my friends . . . because I choose to surround myself with positive people.

One technique I use is meditation. I know, some of you will say you can't turn your brain off and it's impossible to meditate. I understand it isn't always easy, but it will drastically improve your overall state of mind each day. There are several tools available to assist in achieving this state of mind. The goal is to get your mind into an alpha state. Then the creative juices start to bubble up. Ever wonder why you have great ideas in the shower? There are few places to naturally get into an alpha state and water is one of them. I know you can't stand in the shower all day, but be conscious and aware. Take longer showers in the morning and see what happens to your creative juices. For more information, go to www.HowtoCatchAShark.com and click on Resources.

Aim to meditate at least five times each a week. This will help keep your mind clear and will assist you in focusing. It's also is a great way to get in a state of "flow" where things are happening for you at an accelerated pace. In this state, you find that you are able to do two or three times as much work in a fraction of the time it would normally take. When you learn to get yourself into a state of flow, almost on command, you can truly catapult your performance, output and results.

Tell a Great Story

You really need to be able to tell a great story with enthusiasm. Many people get caught up in the detail and numbers forgetting the passion they had for their business and why they started it in the first place. Enthusiasm is infectious.

People love my stories. Why? Not because I have better experiences than others. Rather, because I tell every story with such enthusiasm and excitement. I infuse my personality into every one of my stories. No matter how trivial, tiny or compelling the story is. Each one gets the same Aussie personality.

I focus on living in the now. So, when I tell a story, I'm actually reliving it in that moment and feel like I'm experiencing it for the first time. The times when my story or message has not translated how I hoped, I realized I was looking for an outcome rather than living in the moment.

What's your personality and how can you ensure you are infusing it into every story you tell? Stories told with enthusiasm will make people want to listen more, stay tuned in longer, and be more likely to share the story with others. Which, in turn, helps to extend your brand.

Understand Your Audience

As the storyteller, it's important to understand your audience. Too many people deliver a one-size-fits-all presentation and miss the opportunity to connect with the people they are trying to inspire.

Your story is just as important as understanding body language. People are often fascinated when I share some insight into body language. I want to point out some specifics important when fishing for a Shark.

- Handshake – if someone shakes your hand when you are finished with your presentation and he looks down while he is shaking your hand, that it typically means he didn't believe a word you said or he himself is being dishonest.

- Bring hands together and clasp them – if a person does this while they are presenting, it usually means they wish their Mom or Dad were there. So instead of going in for the "kill" it makes more sense to come in with empathy.

- Eyes looking up or down when speaking – this can determine a lie or whether they are just recalling

- Wiping the back of their neck while answering a question is often a lie.

Refer to my website www.HowToCatchAShark.com for more interesting facts about body language and how to recognize, and in fact use it, to your advantage.

Add Value

Do you or your product solve a problem, transform a situation or add value in some way? Many people get caught up in their own 'story' and forget that all the Shark or customer really wants to know is 'what's in it for me?' Always start with the value you offer rather than the history of what you have done or what the company has achieved in the past. Always look at how you or your company can add the most value to your audience.

In all the ventures I share with Kevin Harrington, the first thing I do is look to how I can add value to him first. I only present him with solutions and exciting updates. I value his knowledge and creativity, and I want to keep him in the place I know he is most effective and valuable. I'm always enthusiastic and never negative no matter whom I deal with.

Intuition

It's important to use your intuition when meeting new people. You can read books and watch programs. But, if you're not physically out there engaging and understanding the people you're dealing with, major opportunities will be missed. At times it can be laborious, especially when some people don't excite you, are closed off, or their interests don't match yours. But when you do find those valuable relationships, every second nurturing it will benefit you and your business.

Have you ever sat through was a boring presentation, but at the end of it walked away with a "light bulb" moment? You know, that one nugget of advice you walked away with making it worth sitting through the boring presentation.

Another piece of advice: Don't go out looking for what you can get from the process. Look for the message you can learn from every conversation, even the challenging ones. Decipher the messages you hear today from others. Can something said be used as another tool for your business? It all pays off when let's say six months down the road that "tool" is exactly what you need to close a business deal. You will immediately reflect, "Oh, that's right, I spoke to John, and he was very similar." Now you've got some knowledge of that personality type. Take an interest in everybody you meet, and understand what you like and don't like to get on top of your intuition. I don't think guys have the same intuitive process women do, but if you work really, really hard on that, you can master it and use it to your advantage. Don't lie to yourself and pretend to be interested. You have to genuinely care enough to find out more, something of value to use, even if it isn't apparent at first. You have to want to know more about them, rather than telling them more about you. The more you start to genuinely understand someone, the more value you take away from the interaction. Be present in the moment always.

Transparency

One of my biggest observations living in America is this: if you can go into a conversation and be completely transparent and practice active listening, you can actually feel the relationship start to get a little bit easier. I feel in America there's a lot of resistance with trust. Speaking as someone from the Australian culture, I think we tend to trust people right away and then if the person messes up the relationship, it's their loss. Generally speaking, Americans take a little more time to trust each other, creating many hoops to go through before building a relationship. But once you do, it's great. Once trust is obtained, Americans are very loyal.

The deals I finish within weeks or months, will often take months or years for some Americans because they have to wait for proof of trust, loyalty, and credibility. I'm not saying to be naïve and silly with your trust, but if you can say what you mean and mean what you say, deliver on time, and expect that in return, you're in. That's really the most simplified process of quickly getting a strategic partner offering. Then, all of the sudden your deals really start to flow quickly. Simply delivering on a promise can make you stand out significantly, and ultimately open doors that would be otherwise closed.

A Personal Story: The Wrong Way to Form a Partnership

Picture this: it was one of the first events I went to with Kevin Harrington. We were standing at the back of the room watching Kevin's 4-minute reel play out on the big screen. The audience didn't know Kevin was actually there.

At the end of the reel, the emcee told the audience that Kevin was at the back of the room and available for a photograph and autograph. You can imagine the reaction . . . 88 people in the room (each of whom paid a premium just to get in) and not a single one of them left before getting a photo or autograph! The line went forever and some people missed out on their lunch break just to meet him.

The Mistake

As flattering as that is for Kevin, if you want to capture your Shark you have to do exactly what everyone else *isn't* doing. I have never heard Kevin speak of meeting a business partner while they were lining up to get a photo or autograph from him. As I say to my kids, "If you follow the crowd you will always end up at the exit."

What You Should Do Instead

In the same situation, I would have approached the person running the event and requested a private introduction to Kevin to put forward my value proposition. I fully believe the only way a Shark is going to listen to you and appreciate your value is through a personal introduction or doing something that sets you apart from the rest.

Until you can approach a Shark as an equal, you're not ready to catch one. Sharks meet so many people and have so many requests placed on their time. In order to capture your Shark and have them see you as a peer, you need to begin acting as a peer and not a fan. Don't put them on a pedestal. Sharks are people too!

Another Example

I recently saw another example of what not to do. Kevin often forwards emails from people wanting to connect with him if he thinks I may be able to add value. Because Kevin is who he is, he always wants to ensure that people who connect directly to him receive a response and help if he can provide it.

This email, though, was pretty rough. It went something like this:

> *"Hi Kevin,*
>
> *I am a successful business executive living in L.A., and I heard you on the radio today on my way to work. I have an idea for a new business and I would love to get together with you to get your thoughts on my concept along with some much-needed advice . . ."*

He was asking Kevin to take time out of his schedule to "help" him—wow! No offer of value he could provide Kevin with, just a request for Kevin's free time! This is not the way to catch a Shark!

I've had the same experience with people approaching me, asking for help with their business with no added value in return. Not that I had any expectations of something in return, but this creates a one-sided business relationship. Mutual added value provides an opportunity for future deals with your Shark.

As I have suggested constantly throughout this book, I believe the key to successful partnerships (whether they be with a Shark or your spouse) is to operate from a place of giving more than you expect in return.

When It's Right, You'll Know

Here's a short story to show you what I mean about getting it right. It's about finding a strategic partner, but the same thing can apply to Sharks.

One of the strategic partners that I brought into my company lives in New York. While putting a deal together, we knew we needed to catch up, so my family and I drove two days to New York to have lunch with him. He was impressed by my commitment to drive two days just for a lunch.

During the visit we took our families to a shopping mall. While our kids shopped, we sat on a park bench and become engaged in a conversation about business and how challenging it can be. My partner asked me how I handle it. I decided to tell him the following story about my daughter.

I have three children, all of whom had just changed schools and didn't know anybody. My 5th grade daughter made the volleyball team, without ever having played previously. She developed new friendships and was "ON FYRE." She was so excited and all the kids loved her. She has a great personality and was really becoming very good at the sport. One day the teacher split the girls into two teams, 6th graders and 5th graders. When the 5th graders were finished with their last game, there was still one game left for the 6th graders to play.

The coach, very young and inexperienced, decided to get both teams together and pick one team out of it. Her goal was to only have the 6th graders play, but three of the girls couldn't play for various reasons. My daughter's three closest friends from the 5th grade were chosen to take a place on the team, leaving my daughter as the only one left out.

She was so devastated and upset when she came home. From a dad's perspective, my heart has never been broken so badly. I didn't think I could ever feel so much pain. It was only a volleyball game, but it meant so much to her. She felt her peers were now looking at her like she's not good enough, and that it would cause her to lose friends. I sat her down on the front porch (or veranda as we would say in Australia). And, although I already knew the answer, I asked, "Isabella, how many 5th grade kids didn't make the team?"

"Dad, I was the only one," she said sobbing.

"Do you understand that these pains you are going through right now, the other three girls are not going through? That means that this is making you stronger. OMG Isabella, you have just received a special gift!" I said with excitement.

Tears stopped and her eyes widened as she said, "Dad, you are so happy. I don't understand."

I said, "Well think about this: there's something bigger and better that's going to happen very soon with you, and this pain right now is happening for a reason. So maybe one day you will be able to help someone else deal with a similar situation. These other girls won't be in a position to be able to deal with what's coming. So, whatever the universe is telling you right now, it's saying, 'Don't worry about it.' You have to harden up right now. I know it hurts, but it's going to make you stronger, and you're going to become a better person out of this experience."

My strategic partner and I both got a little emotional when I told him this story. We hugged and thanked each other for the support. From that moment, we went from being strategic partners to close friends. We're in business together right now. He knows that if we reach any difficult moments in our business, I'm going to be there in the trenches with him. All leaders are "ON FYRE" when the wind is behind them. It's when fighting against the wind you have to step up and start finding out who you are. That's when real leadership comes into play.

I always assure my partners being in business with me is going to be fun! They KNOW I'll go above and beyond to make sure the business is successful. Adding this sort of value is the type of thing you have to do when you are in business looking for strategic partners.

SHARK BITE

by Kevin Harington

Sharks Won't Eat It

There is one main thing that you should avoid when trying to catch a Shark . . . it's the "me, me, me" way of thinking. Avoid saying "I this, I that, I have." It has to initially be about why the Shark should listen to you. Too many people are focused on "I'm the best and I'm this and I'm that." Forgo the mentality of thinking everybody's going to want your product, because at the end of the day, not everybody will. Initially your presentation must distinguish why the Shark should listen to you in the first place. In order to take the next step, you have to convince the Shark WHY you're even worth doing business with.

A big turnoff is people saying they are going invent something much better than the iPhone. There are a billion cellular phones out there. Here is the usual pitch: "If we only get 10% of the market, we're going sell a hundred million of them. But let's say that 10% is too high. Let's say we only get 1% of the telephone market. We're still going to sell 10 million phones." This is just projection, it means nothing. When people spout this, most Sharks will swim away. It's surprising how many use this in their presentation.

Sharks do want to know what the market size is, but avoid saying, "If we only get 1% of the market, then we're all going to be wealthy." 1% of the (cell phone example) market is impossible to get. Samsung can get it, but you need to show a Shark all the reasons why *you're* going to get it. Not just a blanket statement.

Strategic Partners

Coming from widespread success in Australia, we wanted to take it to the next level with Hydrodog and compete with the American dog grooming market. We put together a team, acquired business partners, raised capital, and got the Big Blue Dog built in the U.S. Our trailers, which we designed to wash the dogs in and to make us stand out from the crowd, were a huge replica of an actual toy dog in the color blue.

In order to launch effectively, we needed to have strategic partners.

I became very good friends with the Vice President of the Franchise Council of America, IFA (International Franchise Association). He set me up with some very influential connections in the industry, which gave me the opportunity to start piecing together the U.S. franchise model. Dealing with each state is like dealing with an individual country. It was a minefield of red tape for me. In Australia, you have one franchise agreement that covers all seven states and territories.

This is not the case in the U.S. You can have many different agreements because it varies by state and territory. The master agreement must be structured in a specific way as well. I had to learn pretty fast and needed to find an expert in the legal franchise arena.

I knew it wasn't just about having the business model, or understanding the industry. It was about understanding the regulatory and legal aspects of franchising in America. So, I handpicked two guys out of a group of four individual meetings and worked with the ones I was most congruent with.

Strategic Partners Help You Find Your Shark

A strategic partner is somebody that can help you achieve a higher level of business in an area that's not your expertise. It is somebody better than you at what they do, and can influence the marketplace, introducing you to the right people.

Strategic partners are often found, not necessarily through networking, but through finding out who is already in the space you're interested in, and developing a relationship with them. If you're putting together a team and building a business, you want to be able to streamline, so you search for the type of person to help you do that. Often, it's somebody you know, or somebody that can introduce you to them. The strategic partner lays down the platform, often directing you toward the Shark you are looking for.

Fortune 500 companies have been doing it for years. Strategic partnerships are formed to provide a mutually beneficial alliance between two or more businesses or entrepreneurs.

Bigger companies have more resources than smaller businesses. Strategic partnerships can help them compete effectively with larger firms by leveling the playing field.

A Strategic Partner vs. A Shark

A strategic partner at times can be more important than a Shark because the strategic partner helps to establish the foundation of the business model to attract the Shark. If I was in a business on my own and went out searching for a Shark straight away, I could be viewed as a one-man show. But if I go out, backed by strategic partnerships, it lends credibility. It shows trust, loyalty and belief in the business. Then, all of a sudden, the Shark does his homework and thinks, "Well, this guy is well-connected, and has some great business partners." He takes a more serious look at what the business model is.

Coming to America, I had to make it about *we*, rather than *me*. I strategically went out to find the right partnerships that could lead me to my Shark. When you turn your business from *me* to *we*, the exponential growth is amazing. I think there is a misconception about holding on to 100% of your company and employing other people. Although there are some exceptions, your employees are not necessarily going to give your company the commitment that partners who have equity (sweat equity or financial investment) will. I always make sure I've got full control of my company, but great leverage having a team of expert strategic partners.

The strategic partner needs to be respected by the Shark. They don't necessarily need to work together because you're the one looking for the Shark relationship. The strategic partner needs to be a respected part of the overall team. Ultimately, it's about YOU having the direct correlation with the Shark in order to take it to the next level.

How Many Strategic Partners?

The number of strategic partnerships largely depends on the size of the business and your need for other expertise. You're the leader and founder. You're the one who runs the organization and makes the decisions. You control the strategic partnership. This partnership allows you to focus on the big picture and direction of the company, confident you have congruent partners taking care of their areas of expertise.

I learned the value of strategic partnerships very early in life playing Rugby League in Australia. As a front row (or prop forward), my job was to smash through the defense of the opposing team to move the ball and team forward and closer to the try line (goal). Each of the 13 players on the field had very different roles and skill sets. Playing Rugby League taught me to value my own strengths and appreciate the strengths and skills of the other team members and the fact that it takes more than one person to create magic. Without the collaborative approach and varying skill set of each player, the team would not be effective.

Types of Strategic Partners

There are different types of strategic partners and depending on your business age and size you may require all or some to help take your business to the next level:

Strategic Financial Partners

Strategic financial partners can be bankers, financial investors and financial advisors. Teaming with strategic financial partners can help you fund and manage the financial resources of your company.

Strategic Marketing Partners

Marketing is one of the most important aspects of your business. Forming effective strategic marketing alliances can add enormous value. Whether it is an alliance with a company who has a similar demographic reach to yours or partnership with a marketing firm, strategic marketing partnerships are a great way to get your business out there with minimal upfront cost.

Some examples of successful strategic Marketing partnerships include:

Starbucks

Starbucks partnered with Barnes and Noble bookstores in 1993 to provide Starbucks coffee shops inside every store. Both companies benefited from a mutual demographic. In 1996, Starbucks partnered with PepsiCo to bottle, distribute and sell the popular coffee-based drink, Frappuccino. Starbucks and United Airlines have also partnered resulting in Starbucks coffee being served on all United Airlines flights. A partnering with Kraft foods has resulted in Starbucks coffee being marketed in grocery stores.

Jaguar

Understanding that they shared a similar demographic, Jaguar partnered with Playboy to throw a party at Pebble Beach. Stuart Schorr, VP of Communications for Jaguar Land Rover in North America says, "Owners of Jaguar cars like an upscale, but relaxed and fun environment. Playboy reaches an obviously male target, but it also represents a fun, sexy lifestyle that aligns with our view of a great evening." Playboy helps to keep Jaguar fresh and current, while Jaguar lends a touch of class and tradition to Playboy's brand.

Strategic Suppliers

From manufacturing to office supplies to suppliers of services, forming strategic supply partnerships enable you to run efficiently with ample supplies distributed in a timely manner and at minimal cost. Having strategic relationships in this area can also result in acquiring certain supplies tailored to your company's specific needs.

Microsoft relies on strategic vendor-supplier relationships with key hardware designers such as Dell, Hewlett Packard, Compaq, and IBM.

Department stores such as Macy's no longer own their inventory; the brand occupying the space runs the department in which they are located.

Strategic Technology Partners

Strategic technology partners can be website designers, network administrators, computer repair and service professionals, or SEO and social media experts. Having strategic technology partnerships can give your company a competitive advantage by ensuring your company stays current with technology by tailoring technologies to benefit your company's requirements.

Hydrodog's Strategic Partners

When bringing Hydrodog to the U.S., I initially required strategic partnerships in the form of manufacturing and franchise establishment. I needed to align myself with people who were experts in U.S. franchise law and understood the rules and regulations.

One component was the franchise attorney, and the other was the franchise consultant. In addition to strategy consulting, the franchise consultant puts together the training manuals and documentation to accompany the franchise disclosure document, otherwise known as the FDD. These two blokes were the initial strategic partners I aligned myself with in order to conquer franchising in America. We now have several businesses together from franchising to consulting.

From a manufacturing perspective, I created a strategic supply relationship with our manufacturer, which resulted in keeping costs low and providing them with the comfort of exclusivity and minimum order requirements.

Once you take the relationship away from a strict monetary transaction and start to think about creative ways of ensuring a win-win, the relationship goes to the next level.

SHARK HUNTER TIDBITS

1. Make sure you are congruent with a person before trying to enter into business together. Everybody has that gut feeling when they meet someone. If you aren't comfortable or interested in how the person is right away, it's not a good sign.

2. Adopt a "we" verses a "me" attitude. Think about what you can give rather than what you can get. Be interesting . . . it's extremely powerful and will add value.

3. Get creative. Do something no one has ever done before.

4. Be your authentic self ALWAYS!

5. Be consistent in the manner in which you deal with people.

CH🦈PTER 6

SWIMMING IN
THE SHARK SCHOOL

———— ❧ ☙ ————

P eople often ask me about the relationship I have with my Shark and how it has enhanced my business. The aim of this chapter is to outline the flow of the connections and business opportunities I have created since joining forces with Kevin.

Shark Business Adventures

Bellebrations is an exciting business concept my wife and I created after seeing a similar product in Australia. The idea is traditional wedding bells with a unique computer system to ring multiple bells at one time. Between my franchise experience/knowledge and Kevin's creativity/celebrity/business contacts, we realized we could expand this business internationally.

Kevin immediately introduced me to a extremely well connected family in NYC who founded a nationally recognized and well-established jewelry line. They've been on QVC for 25 years as well as having stores across the country. They are a very powerful and well-respected family.

Kevin invited one of the family members and managing partner of the company to an event I was speaking at. I met him briefly at the event and we had instant rapport. A few weeks later I flew to NYC to catch up with him and discuss our Bellebrations brand and quickly realized we were "cut from the same cloth." He embodied everything I look for in an ideal partner. From his value system to his transparency, I knew we would work well together.

From there I was introduced to one of his business partners who just happened to be a PR guru to the stars! She was able to open doors for us in NYC to have our launch at the Knot Gala on the steps of the New York Library!

The Ripple Effect Continues . . .

The celebrity PR guru and our jewelry tycoon joined forces and became a part of the Bellebrations team in NYC. They then introduced me to the event coordinator of the Knot Gala (who happens to be one of the most influential celebrity wedding planners and personalities in the industry). He is also now a strategic partner in our company.

We now have created a foundation of incredibly high profiled people in our business adding enormous credibility.

A foundation such as this enabled me to join forces with one of the #1 wedding venues in the U.S. Together we have become strategic partners adding mutual value and creating a new business model incorporating both of our businesses. We have also met who we consider to be extended family through this connection. It's really incredible how a small introduction to the right person or people can have such a snowball effect and change lives.

Kevin and I laugh about the fact he doesn't need to open a door anymore. All I need is a small crack in a window and I will take it from there! I think that's the key to why we work so well together. This is also an important thing to remember when dealing with your Shark. Kevin is always blown away with my ability to connect and he is proud to have me as a business partner. If you are not on that level with your Shark, your relationship will only ever be temporary.

Since meeting, Kevin and I are involved in several business ventures. Some I have brought to him and others he has introduced. We have criteria to which we strictly adhere to and if the business or idea doesn't fit, we don't proceed. We value our friendship above all and will only jump into opportunities together that will enhance our friendship, and complement our value system and each other's strength as a team.

A mate of mine invited me to attend his professional speaking course. We formed a mutual respect for each other and during a casual conversation over coffee, he mentioned to me he was affiliated in some way with a business development company from the UK who referenced my Hydrodog success and me throughout their program. He went on to say how they would love to bring their program (which was a huge success in the UK and Australia) to the U.S.. He acknowledged as great as he is at his craft, he is by no means equipped to even think about how to bring a company from the UK to the U.S. Within a week of our discussions I was on a plane headed to the UK to meet the founders of this company. I must say that my initial attraction was the fact that they were two blokes from Australia and I wanted to help them bring their business over and avoid the pitfalls I endured.

The founders and I hit it off immediately; they knew of me from Australia, however we had never previously crossed paths. I told them I would help them in any way I could to get to the U.S. Their business model was not an industry that I was familiar with but saw the potential for a franchise. Knowing Kevin's background, knowledge and especially his connections in this industry, I knew he would be able to add value and may be interested in being part of this deal. I called him from the UK and told him to "buckle up!" "I have an amazing opportunity! Let's chat when I get home," I said. By the time I arrived back in the U.S., Kevin had already read the founders book and had done his research on the company and said to me, "Buddy, let's do this."

I immediately took action and we brought their company to the U.S. and successfully launched Key Person of Influence U.S.

Although Hydrodog and Bellebrations was the original reason for me capturing my Shark, our partnership has expanded well beyond those two businesses.

I strongly believe that if after capturing your Shark you don't become one, you have not truly benefited from the relationship.

How Important Is Friendship in Business?

Certain Sharks may require friendship. I am that Shark. I don't want to be a partner with somebody I wouldn't want to have over to my house for Thanksgiving dinner. For me, it's more than business and I want only to be aligned with people of similar values.

Ultimately, this is my style and I know it's Kevin's style as well. But a lot of Sharks, like Kevin O'Leary, don't care about Thanksgiving dinner. He wants to spend Thanksgiving dinner with HIS family and not yours. But that's just him. I'm the kind of guy who believes it could be a much bigger relationship if developed. I know Kevin feels the same having spent Christmas with his family. I want to be around empowering people. It's not only good for my personal life, but for business too. If you're working with happy and motivated people, deals are going to come to you.

Shark Traits

Of the all the deals Kevin invested in on *Shark Tank*, the most successful ventures were those where the entrepreneur didn't expect Kevin to make it all happen. The entrepreneurs were self-starters and true entrepreneurs. Kevin wouldn't be able to enter into the deals if he was expected to handle the minutia of every business he was involved in.

SHARK BITE

by Kevin Harington

A Meeting with Donald Trump

Twenty-plus years ago, I had a large number of commissioned salespeople working for me. They were all smart guys and smart alecks. They were having a difficult time making sales calls. Donald Trump's book had just come out, *The Art of the Deal*. It was his first book. He was THE big real estate tycoon and my idol at that particular time. So, one day my sales team was complaining they couldn't get through to a client or get anyone on the phone. I replied, "You guys, I can get through to anybody. It's easy. You just have to come up with the right plan to do it."

So they challenged me, "Oh, okay. Tell you what. You got Donald Trump's book on your desk? Get through to Donald Trump, Mr. Smarty Pants."

I'm like, what? *Get through to Donald Trump?* "Okay. I'll get through to Donald Trump."

They laughed, "You're going to get through to him and set up a meeting with him, like you said?"

With confidence I replied, "I'll get a meeting with him. I'll get a meeting with Donald Trump. You guys are challenging me? Let's put some money on it! Give me a week. Seven days."

Now I had to put a plan together.

Donald Trump's book was co-authored by Tony Schwartz. The way to get to Trump isn't by calling Donald Trump, because he's never going to take my call. His secretary would hang up on me. Instead, I called Tony and left a message for him, saying I'd like to sell a million of his books. Do you think he's going to return my call? Yeah, of course he is.

He's going to call me back, because he makes a royalty on the book sales. Let's just say the book costs $25. The co-author is probably making at least a buck a book. So, is he going to return my call? Absolutely. Same day. Within the hour.

When he called me back, I said, "Hey, Kevin Harrington here. I'm thinking I can sell a million of your books."

Tony responds dumfounded, "What? Who are you?"

I replied, "I'm the guy doing the 'As Seen on TV' products and I sell 'How To Make Money in Real Estate' on TV. Who's the biggest guy in real estate? Donald Trump. I can sell a million of your books."

Tony's now on board, "What do we need to do?"

"I need a meeting with Donald."

He responds, "Okay. I'll call you right back."

This was on Monday. When he called me back he had a meeting for me with Donald on Wednesday. I was in front of Trump 48 hours later. That's how quick it happened. In order to catch the Shark, you don't always go right to the Shark. Sometimes, you have to get to the people who can also benefit from the deal cutting them in a little bit. Ultimately, that's the schmoozing it takes to catch the Shark.

I'm scheduled to meet with Donald and Tony (the co-author of the book). We're meeting at Trump Tower in New York. It's a large gold building and there's this big guy, a guard, who greets me when I arrive.

He questions me, "Who are you?"

"I have a meeting with Donald Trump."

He doesn't believe me, "Oh, yeah. Sure you do."

I'm almost a kid. This happened 25 years ago. I persist, "Seriously. I have a meeting with Donald Trump upstairs. He's on the 33rd floor, right?"

"Yeah," he says, "Let me check . . ." Using the receiver in his ear, he calls to verify. "You're Kevin Harrington?"

"Yeah," I say.

"You do have a meeting. Go."

I ride the elevator up to the 33rd floor and the doors open to a reception area. The receptionist says, "Mr. Trump will be right with you. Take a seat over there."

I sit. I'm there waiting and I'm nervous. I sort of had a pitch ready to go, but not really sure what I was going to say. Trump's office door is open. He's IN the office. I'm waiting literally a few feet away from him. I'm sitting there for almost a half-hour. He's screaming at the top of his lungs at someone on the phone, "I told you I said gold, not silver! This is bullshit! I'm going get every penny back from you!"

As I'm listening to him, all I'm thinking is, "I have to come in after this and talk to him!"

Trump slams the phone down, and says, "Get that punk kid in here who came to pitch me something!"

I hear this and the secretary says, "Ha-ha . . . good luck."

I walk into his office and there's a chair sitting in front of his desk. I start to grab the chair to sit down and he screams, "Wait a minute! You're here to pitch me something. I don't know what this deal is or what it's about." He's just really nasty. Trump then says, "Before you sit down. You're pitching me something. I don't know what it is, but it's going take some of my time to do this deal, right?"

I reply, "Well, yes. If you decide you want to do the deal, I'm going to need some of your time."

Trump says, "Well, before you sit down, how much of my time is it going take and how much money could I make on this . . . this deal you're going pitch?"

Hmmm, I think for a second, "First of all, Mr. Trump, I appreciate your time in just allowing me to meet you face to face. I need four hours of your time and you're going make four million dollars if you do this deal I'm about to present to you."

He took about eight seconds to think about it, and then said, "All right. Sit down."

So, that's how a guy like Trump looks at life. I love telling this story because number one, I got the deal. I pitched him a deal and he bit. He bought the deal and he said, "Go. Let's do it."

The deal? I was to create an audio/DVD set on how to make money in real estate. I wanted to put him on TV and shoot an infomercial to say, "I'm Donald Trump and there's no body better than me at making money in real estate and this is how I do it. Here's my course."

He said, "That is absolutely brilliant. I want to do it. Let's do it!" Unfortunately, down the road as we were working on putting it together, some of his people wouldn't let him go on the show. They didn't want him hawking "no money down real estate" at two o'clock in the morning on infomercials. But he did love it and gave me rights to it. He said, "Go do it." So, I got the deal and I got the Shark. I also developed my perfect pitch. My pitch to him was, "I need four hours and you're going to make four million."

True story. This guy was such a barracuda. People often ask me what one of the game changers in my life was. This meeting was definitely one of them. I always think to myself before calls or meetings, "How much of my time is this call/meeting going to take and what's my upside? Or do I move on to the next deal?"

Trump's philosophy is: *I'm going to give you a couple minutes of my time, in that same time frame, I could be on the phone making some money. So you better make my time worth it.*

How much time is your pitch going to take? What's the deal you want me to do? What's my upside? That's how you need to talk to Donald Trump. If you have 30 seconds to tell Donald Trump something like "Hey Donald, I need 30 seconds of your time and it's worth four million dollars to you." He would say, "Let's freaking talk for 30 seconds." You've got to hone your pitch to the person you're dealing with. It has to be specific to the Shark you're trying to catch.

With someone like Warren Buffett, it would be a different story. If you said, "I've got a deal that's going to put 10 million dollars into a trust for your favorite charity," Warren Buffett would like that. If you pitched the same concept to Donald Trump, he would laugh at you and never talk to you again.

SHARK HUNTER TIDBITS

1. Exhaust all avenues to get to your Shark. It's not always a direct route.

2. A Shark can take your business places where it has never been before—contacts "snowball" as you meet more and more people.

3. Long-term relationships are what really build businesses, and congruence is important if you want to have a long-term relationship.

4. Do your research. Discover what makes your Shark tick.

5. Don't expect your Shark to be involved in the day-to-day operation of your business. Respect their strengths and make efficient use of their time.

CHAPTER 7

BRINGING TWO SHARKS TOGETHER

This deal alone is one of my biggest accomplishments in the Shark world to date.

When I brought Key Persons of Influence (KPI) to America, I was introduced to a new social media/events/branding platform. The founder of the company is a bloke by the name of John Bartoletta. John did a pitch in front of my group and I was completely blown away. He was full of passion, excitement and his delivery was second to none. I immediately needed to get to know this guy as I found him to be a powerhouse.

We tried to put a deal together with his company and KPI. For various reasons, the deal did not move forward despite the mutual value we saw in each other's businesses. This is a great example of the value I see in Sharks. I spot the potential of a long-term relationship and I'm relentless to get to know them personally by adding value, not even knowing what the future deal is going to be.

Over the next two years, John and I kept in touch with each other on a regular basis, exchanging advice on certain things in life and business and truly developed a bloody unreal mateship.

In the meantime, my original Shark, Kevin Harrington, started a new company collaborating with a top cell phone provider to have the new company's app on the front screen of over seven million phones. This was a huge win and very exciting for Kevin and his team.

On a recent trip home to Sydney, John called to see what it was like Down Under, wanting an instant photo to confirm how beautiful it really was. He started to tell me they were doing an event and how the UNATION app had been downloaded in record numbers! The penny dropped! I said to Bart (John) "What if I could get UNATION on seven million phones?" Using his words, he "just about flipped out."

All I had to do was bring the Sharks together to pull off an amazing deal.

Bart and Kevin knew each other but didn't have the relationship I had with each individually. Both of these blokes trust me on a very high level, so I became the conduit of the deal.

First, I organized a call for Bart and Kevin to speak, each putting what they had on the table and how it could work bringing their companies together. After their conversation, Kevin rang and told me this could really work. He only had one question. "For this deal to work, it can't take months with all the due diligence. We need to launch in June. On your word and guarantee, is John the right partner to make this happen?" I said, "Yes! He is solid. He will deliver and make this happen." Kevin said, "That's good enough for me."

Bart rings me back after he speaks with Kevin "ON FYRE!" He was so excited and immediately started putting things into place as the COO of the new company was coming to Tampa to finalize the paperwork.

The COO comes in to see John and they start putting the deal together. John leaves the room, calls me and fills me in on the exciting progress. When he told me his name, I instantly recalled our first meeting. It came up that Kevin Harrington was my mate and business partner. He then said he had done a couple of deals with Kevin years ago and would love to get back in his circle. I organized a lunch for the three of us to get the relationship back on track. He then ended up becoming Kevin's right hand man in this new business.

I got the COO on the phone and explained I was the one bridging the deal together and he was thrilled I was part of the team. This is yet another example of how associating with the right people really does pay off.

The following Tuesday at 6:00pm, Bart organized a dinner event at his house with all his partners and board members. Contracts were to be finalized at lunchtime and the news presented to everyone that night to celebrate. The attorney and my mate the COO are in the boardroom together. The attorney began playing a little hard ball. It's now 4:00pm and our dinner is at 6:00pm. John calls me and says, "I'm having trouble with this attorney." I asked for his name and yep, you guessed it, a great mate I'm doing deals with. I had Bart put me on the phone with him and I smoothed things over. Everyone ended up signing and we had the best night ever.

I guess for me to bring my celebrity Shark to the table and a Shark in his own right in his industry, a deal of this magnitude took place on my word. What would have taken months took two weeks . . . that's unheard of in deals with big players.

Being consistent creates loyalty . . . and in turn, enormous trust.

SHARK HUNTER TIDBITS

1. Get comfortable with being uncomfortable. This is the place you will meet the most powerful Sharks.

2. Recognize you may meet your Shark well before a deal takes place. Work on building a relationship and adding value first . . . with or without a deal on the table.

3. Be consistent in your communications and behaviors.

4. Remain open to opportunities without expectations. Opportunity may present itself through unfamiliar channels.

5. Add value . . . add value . . . add value!

CHAPTER 8

CATCHING A SHARK WITHOUT AN INTRODUCTION

A s stated in earlier chapters, a great introduction to a Shark is key. It establishes your credibility on a higher level. So, what if you can't get an introduction after identifying your Shark?

As I began writing *How To Catch a Shark*, I decided to Google other authors/books focusing on the topic of "Sharks." A book appeared in the search results called *Swim With The Sharks Without Being Eaten Alive* by Harvey Mackay. His was the only book on this topic and had been written over 25 years ago.

I immediately began calling my Sharks to ask if they knew Harvey. Each one stated they were "one person away" from knowing him. This wasn't going to work for me, so I tried a different approach.

I ordered his book online and in the mail I received a

cassette tape. Yes, I was sent a cassette tape by mistake! I turned the house upside down trying to find a tape recorder. To my amazement I found one! (As I was inserting the tape into the recorder, my son asked, "What's that, Dad?" He'd never seen a cassette tape before! It was a great teaching moment to share a little bit of history with him about something he had never heard of or seen before).

So, I prepared the tape and recorder, along with some headphones. Five days a week for a month I listened to the tape at the gym. It felt like Harvey was talking to me each session and boy did I learn a thing or two.

I began to understand how he influenced top CEO'S and owners (Sharks) to buy products from his company Mackay Envelopes.

The three big takeaways from these tapes were:

1. Harvey Mackay would ask the secretary or personal assistant of CEOs/Owners if he could have 300 seconds of their time to make his pitch.

2. If he went over the 300 seconds, he would donate $500 to a charity of their choice.

3. Harvey Mackay is a massive sports fan.

The last thing Harvey Mackay says on the tape is, "In years to come, someone will undoubtedly update the messages and concepts of this tape. I'll bet that several listeners will be on that roster of future legends. If you have the will and the spirit, why shouldn't you be one of them?"

Harvey Mackay predicted the future and here I am!

I was now ready to put my plan into place to catch the Godfather of Sharks without an introduction. I was armed with his sweet spots and ready to take action!

The first thing I did was ask a mate of mine who owns my old professional rugby league team in Australia called the Titans (formally known as the Seagulls) if I could get a fully signed jersey from all the players. When the jersey arrived, I packaged it with a handwritten note outlining who I was and why I wanted to meet him. And, you guessed it . . . I added a $500 check in the package made out to Harvey's favorite charity (Salvation Army).

I adhered to the same principles I would have with an introduction. I identified the Shark and I added value first.

Once I sent the package, I waited a week then called Harvey's office. I got to his assistant. I introduced myself and he told me I was the talk of the office! Can you imagine how "ON FYRE" I was about that?

His assistant told me Mr. Mackay was out of the office for the next month as he was recording a new series.

However, he sent me a photo of Harvey wearing the jersey I sent!

The plan for this book was to be in print during the month of Harvey's absence. So, check our website www.HowToCatchAShark.com for the outcome of this story!

SHARK HUNTER TIDBITS

1. The biggest mistake when trying to catch your dream Shark is *not* believing it's possible.

2. Any Shark can be caught. All it requires is the right bait and most importantly, fishing for the right Shark in the right waters.

3. Follow the clues Sharks often leave, giving you insight into their sweet spots.

4. Think outside the box and then outside the box again! Get creative.

5. Be confident. Confident people are attracted to confidence.

CHAPTER 9

CATCHING
THE WRONG SHARK

⟶ ❧ ⟵

Earlier in the book I mentioned how Hydrodog started, how it was sold in Australia and then how we brought it to the U.S. Since I began writing this book, something incredible has taken place with Hydrodog.

When we came to America in 2010, I was looking to get Hydrodog USA up and running. There was so much I didn't know when we arrived. After working with my first Shark, it is now very clear. The Hydrodog USA deal took longer than I expected to come together. It was not finalized until 2011.

This is one of the most important lessons I teach . . . catching the wrong Shark. I wasn't feeling congruent with my own philosophy. I still added value, but didn't jump out of bed excited and "ON FYRE" to work with this group.

A lot of money was spent creating the infrastructure to franchise the business. All we needed to do was duplicate the process we used in Australia, and we were on track to do so.

I went back to Australia for a funeral and when I got back to the U.S., the team had decided not to franchise anymore and wanted to corporatize the company. Now that's the last thing I wanted to be a part of, so we put a buyout together.

Hydrodog in Australia was and is still very successful. We had created a working franchise system. But it didn't start out this way. When first starting the company, I used an employee model and it nearly sent us broke. There were a few hitches we became aware of: when it rains, the operators don't get out of bed; when they get on the piss (get drunk) on a Friday night, they don't turn up for work on Saturday. Most importantly, they all leave the customers in the lurch.

After expressing this concern to the team I built in the U.S., they still believed they could put in their own infrastructure solving the issues/problems I felt so strongly opposed to. I knew it wouldn't work for me, so we decided to part ways and opt for a buyout.

One thing I am so thankful for is having my children sitting at the boardroom table as I finalized the buyout. They were only 10, 9 and 8 years of age at the time! It was one of those bloody unreal moments in life because the kids were seeing a real transaction in business take place and watching their Dad in action. It really was a proud moment and the kids were amazing.

After about 3 months, I began wearing my Hydrodog shirt around the house again. Then, my beautiful wife followed suit. Even my oldest daughter would wear one to bed. I was sending the message I would get Hydrodog back one day.

Nearly 18 months after the buyout, I received a call inquiring about any interest I had in buying back the business. Of course, I was excited way beyond comprehension as this business was my baby.

After going back and forth for a couple of months, we finally came to an agreement. The purchase was pennies on the dollar and truly a great deal.

One of the biggest lessons still resonating with me today is the fact I never burned any bridges. When it was time to work together for the best end result, I must say, it was an absolute pleasure doing business with them.

It was now time to put a team together. Then out of the blue this bloke rings me. He had used Hydrodog in the past to groom his service dogs. His lovely wife had hunted me down and then he pestered me like you wouldn't believe to keep him in mind once I reclaimed the business (he was very persistent). I assumed he only wanted to purchase a franchise. Little did I know he had a business partner who understood Enterprise Resource Planning (ERP) and internet elements needed to run very successful multi-national companies. They were both interested in more than just a franchise.

At this point, I had four different options to create teams for the ""new Hydrodog" (I felt very blessed). My goal was to find partners for Hydrodog displaying skills I didn't have or didn't like to perform. These two blokes were my perfect matches. At the same time, I did not forget about my first Shark Kevin Harrington and our own in house attorney. I am happy to say they are also partners in Hydrodog USA.

After we secured Hydrodog and the team, it was time to work on restoring the name and figure out how to acquire national coverage with a bang.

Late one night while I was in a deep sleep, my beautiful wife woke me up and said, "I've got it!" Still half asleep, I heard myself saying, "What have you got (to be honest, I thought I was getting lucky)? With excitement she said, "Let's get a big RV to tow the Big Blue Dog around the country washing dogs and saving lives at all the shelters."

A light bulb went on! I immediately started to put things into place. The Bathe to Save Tour was born.

SHARK HUNTER TIDBITS

1. Never burn a bridge.

2. Stay true to your value system.

3. Understand your non-negotiables and know when it's time to exit the relationship.

4. Great energy attracts great energy. Always deliver your "ON FYRE" self!

5. Business partners should have the same passion for your business as you do. Look for complementary skill sets to your own.

CHAPTER 10

THE BATHE TO SAVE TOUR

O ur commitment to the U.S. tour is so huge we took the kids out of conventional school and now have them doing what's called "school of the air" in Australia. It's a program for kids living in the Australian Outback or overseas unable to attend school because of the distance. The opportunity for our kids to be heavily involved in giving back for a charity of this magnitude and understanding the social conscience side is going to be a true gift for them . . . actually, for all of us.

When we first came to the U.S., we didn't know anyone. Fast forward a few years, we were very settled in a great house, school for the kids and had made amazing friends. Everything felt like home and we were certainly very comfortable. Then we decided to embark on something very foreign to us . . . an 18-month, 50-state and over 300 city excursion around the U.S. to raise awareness of the multiple benefits of animal adoption.

We want to save dogs lives. By transporting the big blue Hydrodog mobile grooming unit to every state behind our huge house on wheels, the Bathe To Save Team aims to wash 25,000 dogs raising one million dollars with 100 percent of the proceeds going directly to the local shelters. Along the way we will visit all the historical landmarks of this beautiful country and teach our children the value of giving back. Since only 30% of pets in homes are adopted from shelters, we felt the need to raise awareness.

Our national tour, Bathe to Save (www.BathetoSave. com), was only possible due to the relationships we had been able to attract during our three years in the U.S. Together with a group of amazing entrepreneurial sponsors, we are able to give back to the industry we are so passionate about . . . this is our mission and goal!

Recently I was asked to speak about taking risks to a group of entrepreneurs. I said to the bloke heading up the class, Mr. Tye Maner (what a champion), I didn't see it as taking risks in entrepreneurship. It's been uncomfortable and I have burned ships behind me. To me, that's the big difference in being a true entrepreneur. Don't confuse *burning bridges* with *burning your ships behind you*. Burning a bridge is destroying a relationship beyond repair that was more than likely a healthy one at some point. *Burning your ships behind you* comes from the story of Hernán Cortés, a Spanish Conquistador leading an expedition to the New World in the 16th century. Upon arrival, Cortés gave an order to burn all ships, making a clear statement to his men . . . there is no turning back now. Two years later he and his men brought down the Aztec Empire. This piece of history and its lesson still remains relevant today. To be a great leader, assure your team the avenue during challenges is always forward.

Moving from Australia to the U.S. was extremely uncomfortable and yes, we burned all our ships behind us. But to me, the risk didn't exist. I couldn't fail and I had a Big Blue Dog!

The transition from our home to a home on wheels was interesting to say the least! Wow! What an adventure getting to know this world of RV parks and RV living. Although we have a large RV, there still was not a great deal of room left after my beautiful wife's clothes and shoes were accommodated!

A great mate of mine (world MMA champion) came up with the phrase, "I'm comfortable being uncomfortable." The penny dropped for me once I heard those words. When you see uncomfortable coming, embrace it and your life will never be the same again.

I am so grateful for having the best of the best around me at all times and this Bathe To Save Tour is no different. This can only happen if you're authentic, consistent and continually adding value. My congruency with each company and every person involved is mind blowing.

Visit our website www.BatheToSave.com to take a look at our amazing sponsors, both corporations and individuals. Through their various skill sets and contributions, they have helped make this tour a reality.

The U.S. Bathe To Save Tour doesn't end when we reach our goal over the next 18 months. We didn't want to be a "one trick wonder" after saving so many canine lives! No doubt we are going to create massive awareness, but what happens after the tour? Well, let me tell you!

Every time a Hydrodog franchise is sold, the new franchise owner will be encouraged to have a "Dog Wash Day" once a month at their local shelter to raise money for saving the lives of so many dogs.

For example, if each franchise saves five dogs a month and we have 100 franchises, Hydrodog will be saving 500 dogs a month! Wow! Let's say over the next few years we have 1,000 franchises saving five lives a month. That's 5,000 lives per month. Deadset amazing and mind blowing! And, in combination with other charities, we could eradicate euthanasia! It is of the utmost importance for Hydrodog to recruit the best franchisees in order to create a likeminded culture all sharing the same goals.

If you want to follow this crazy Aussie family's adventures, you will be able to with a tracking app. There will be regular blog posts from Bubbles, a rescue dog we will be adopting on our launch day here in

Tampa! The kids are going to be the voice of Bubbles via social media. Bubbles will be our official mascot.

My next book will be written beginning with the first day of the tour. My family and I will be documenting our experiences and adventures as we trek across the U.S. for 18 months. Of course, it will include all the Sharks we meet along the way!

SHARK HUNTER TIDBITS

1. Identify your mission and your "why."

2. Be prepared to burn your ships behind you. A great leader provides no avenues for retreat.

3. Step out of your comfort zone. This is where extraordinary deals may occur.

4. Believe in your mission and believe in yourself.

5. Don't do your best . . . rise to a higher level than you ever expected.

SHARK BITE

FINAL THOUGHTS: Kevin Harrington

The last three years Anthony and I have been business partners and friends has been a riot. The thing about our partnership that makes it different than any other business relationship is we have a ton of fun. A day in our lives is beyond amazing. The fact we can do deals, meet other celebrities and have a blast all at once is what life is all about. Tying these three aspects together is what makes it dynamic.

The other great thing about Anthony is, since he knows me so well, he only brings deals beneficial for both of us. He doesn't waste my time with crappy stuff. He knows my busy schedule and can tell if I'm not "feeling" a particular situation. This makes all of our meetings and business deals solid. We trust one another, and he brings solutions, not problems, to the table.

An example of a typical day with Anthony:

I'm at a party with high-end business people. We're talking billionaires here. It's also full of NFL football players, movie stars and reality celebrities; we're rubbing elbows with the elite. I think to myself that Anthony needs to be here because he's such a boisterous personality; he would just fit in and make some great connections. So I text Anthony and tell him to come over because I have some people he needs to meet. Bam!

30 minutes later, he's there. He was not star struck with anyone in the room and was able to be his "Australian self" cracking jokes and being silly. Everybody falls in love with him and deals start falling together.

Anthony's got this hilarious personality that really taps into mine. I definitely live vicariously through him. He's a little bit crazy, which I enjoy, and he's definitely not your average person. I feel that's the connection we have because I was a little crazy when I was younger as well and we definitely hit it off. We often say that we're two peas in a pod and like to talk about things that most people don't, things that are just really funny to us. So we're in contact every day. I always get back to him first when I can because I know he's always got something exciting to share. There's nothing he tells me on a daily basis that has any negative connotations or problems.

I love to put the right people together, as far as opening the doors, because my contact database is very significant. Anthony is brilliant at going in and spending quality time with people we can do deals with. We both have our strengths and we fit together like a fine piece of machinery. Everything just clicks right in place and huge million dollar deals are easily constructed. It's really a beautiful thing when you can find that perfect person for your business partner, then the sky is the limit!

I'm sure Anthony's next book will be titled, *How to Become a Shark* because that's exactly what he's become.

Once you catch the Shark for your business, like me, and you develop it as a long-term mutual beneficial relationship, the only way is up. You'll eventually become a Shark in the business ocean and other aspiring entrepreneurs will try to catch you.

FINAL THOUGHTS: Anthony Amos

I wasn't like the typical entrepreneurs featured on *Shark Tank* pitching my business to the panel, trying to get a deal. I was different; I did the research and decided which Shark would benefit my business the most. I decided to focus on Kevin Harrington . . . to make him a part of my business. I knew his brand and contact database would bring my business to the next level. Kevin, being as creative as he is, suggested since I was the one who "caught the Shark," we write a book about my story in order to teach others how to do the same.

I hope you enjoyed our journey together and now know how to catch your Shark and start your business "ON FYRE!" Please feel free to reach out to me at www.HowToCatchAShark.com.

ABOUT THE AUTHOR

Anthony Amos: From Rugby to Hydrodog and beyond

Anthony started his career playing professional rugby straight out of high school in Australia. While playing football, Anthony decided to use his down time to start his own business. At age 21, he founded a mobile dog grooming business. The Hydrodog 'prototype' consisted of a secondhand Hydrodog-bath (special dog bath) strapped on the back of a box trailer! They put an ad in the local newspaper, rented a mobile phone, waiting for it to start ringing!

Within five years, Hydrodog had grown to over 100 franchises across Australia. It was the first franchise of its kind to be in every State and Territory of Australia.

After the 100th franchise milestone was reached, Hydrodog implemented a Master Franchise model taking the franchise system to a whole new level. All state and territories in Australia were sold within an 18-month period.

Amos and his team revolutionized the dog-grooming industry by designing and creating a fiberglass mobile grooming salon in the shape of a Big Blue Dog. To this day, after 12 years, there is no other product like it on the market place. Hydrodog grew to the largest franchise of its kind in the world at that time, receiving 6,000 new customer calls with a revenue of nearly $10 million annually. Anthony, at the age of 28, became one of Australia's youngest millionaires.

In 2006 he decided and it was time to sell Hydrodog Australia and New Zealand. At the time, it sold for a record sum.

After the sale of Hydrodog Australia and New Zealand, Anthony immersed himself in property development. He discovered his passion wasn't in property. In 2010, he decided to move to the U.S. with his beautiful wife and three amazing children (5,6,7) to expand Hydrodog into the American dog grooming market. After two years establishing the business model and getting the Big Blue Dog manufactured in America, Anthony sold his interest in Hydrodog Dog USA. And in 2015, he bought Hydrodog USA back!

In addition to overseeing his own two founding franchise systems and many partnerships in other businesses, Anthony spends his time advising and mentoring other entrepreneurs, teaching them how to take their businesses to the next level and catch their own Shark! Anthony has equity interests in several companies with his Shark Kevin Harrington. His true passions are people and business. Together with a select group of industry specific experts and his unique business training programs, Anthony ensures the businesses he consults with are positioned in the best possible place in the market.

Anthony is also a keynote speaker specializing in Ultimate Partnerships, how to catch a Shark and franchising. And, he is now a published author.

CONTRIBUTING AUTHOR

Kevin Harrington – Inventor of the Infomercial, Original Shark on *Shark Tank* and As Seen on TV Pioneer

Kevin is one of the most successful entrepreneurs of our time.

In 1980, Harrington started The Small Business Center and Franchise America. Kevin, as a real estate and business broker, sold thousands of businesses and then offered one-stop services from accounting to insurance to advertising to finance and more.

While watching television one night in 1984, Harrington noticed the only thing on the television screen at times were color test patterns the stations ran when they had nothing else to air. This gave Kevin the idea to produce the industry's first 30-minute infomercial to fill dead air space. This is how he was coined the "Inventor of the Infomercial."

Since then, he has been involved with over 500 product launches resulting in sales of over $4 billion dollars worldwide and 20 products reaching individual sales of over $100 million. By 1990, Harrington was named one of the 100 best entrepreneurs in the world (by *Entrepreneur Magazine*).

In the mid-80's, he formed Quantum International, which grew to $500 million in sales selling products in 100 countries in 20 languages. He then formed HSN direct in conjunction with Home Shopping Network and soon after, formed Reliant International Media. Kevin also founded As Seen on TV, Inc. and acquired AsSeenOnTV.com, the world's largest website featuring as seen on TV products.

Harrington has worked with some of the biggest celebrities, including Cee Lo Green, Kim Kardashian, Paris Hilton, 50 Cent, Jack LaLane, George Foreman, Frankie Avalon, Paula Abdul, Montel Williams, Chubby Checker, Hulk Hogan, Kris and Bruce Jenner, Tony Little, Billy Mays, and many more.

In 2009, Kevin was selected as one of the original *Shark Tank* Sharks on the ABC hit show. As an innovator and pioneer in the industry, Kevin has been featured on over 150 *Shark Tank* segments over the last six years on both ABC and CNBC.

Kevin is regularly featured as an industry expert in numerous media outlets, including the *NBC Today Show*, *ABC Good Morning America*, *CBS Morning News*, *The View*, *The Wendy Williams Show*, CNBC, *Squawk Box with Jim Kramer*, *The Bethenny Show*, Bloomberg, Fox Business, CNN, MTV, *Entrepreneur Magazine*, Fast Company, Fortune, Inc., *Wall Street Journal*, *New York Times*, and many more.

He went on and founded two global associations – ERA (Electronic Retailers Association), which is now in 45 countries and Young Entrepreneur's Association (now EO – Entrepreneurs Organization), which boasts combined member sales of over $500 billion dollars.

Harrington is on the board of University of South Florida (USF) entrepreneur programs, and teaches regularly. He has also been involved with Moffitt Cancer Research, and is constantly giving back to the community. Harrington's book *Act Now: How I Turn Ideas Into Million-Dollar Products* details his life and achievements in the direct marketing world. His business was used as a class case study for 12 years at Harvard/MIT, illustrating the essential principles of grass-roots entrepreneurship.

TESTIMONY
by Kevin Harrington

———— ❧❧ ————

Anthony Amos possesses insights not found anywhere else. He sees opportunities we innately recognize, but just need to hear it verbalized from someone who sees it too.

As a Shark Investor and an original Shark on the TV program *Shark Tank*, I meet so many people pitching their concepts I can't remember who they all are! It's not often I come across an entrepreneur like Anthony who stands out and is memorable! Let me correct that . . . there *is* no one like Anthony Amos.

I met Anthony through a lifetime friend of mine. This guy is a Shark in his industry and he called saying I had to meet this crazy Aussie he had gotten to know and more importantly, he was one of us!

Anthony is one of the most exciting, honest, zero drama business partners I've ever had. He's full of integrity and genuinely loves people.

Who else would write a book about catching a Shark? I'm in many businesses with Anthony now, and we've put some great deals together. He is one of a kind and very well connected. I can honestly say I have never seen him not "ON FYRE!"

We all need a lift now and then. When you're a business partner and mate (as Anthony would say) of his, there are very few down days when he's around.

SPECIAL THANKS
TO OUR SPONSORS